Errata

The following errors appear in *Northwest Penstemons:*
80 Species of Penstemon *Native to the Pacific Northwest*
by Dee Strickler:

The running footer in parentheses in the lower right-hand corner
of odd-numbered pages 147-183 should read "Anthers dehisce
totally," except on pages 179 and 181. The footer on page 179
is correct as it is, and the footer on page 181 should read
"Anthers may dehisce less than totally."

Northwest Penstemons

80 Species of *Penstemon* Native to the Pacific Northwest

Dee Strickler
Photography and Text

Zoe Strickler
Graphic Design

Anne Morley
Illustrations

Front cover: *Penstemon venustus*
Note: for a description see pages 54–55.

**Dedicated to penstemon lovers
(penstemaniacs) everywhere.**

Library of Congress Catalog Card Number: 97-061340
ISBN 1-56044-572-6

Published by the Flower Press
Columbia Falls, Montana

Publishing Consultant:
SkyHouse Publishers, an imprint of
Falcon® Publishing Company, Inc.,
Helena and Billings, Montana

To order extra copies of this book, contact:
The Flower Press, 192 Larch Lane, Columbia Falls, MT 59912, or
Falcon®, P.O. Box 1718, Helena, MT 59624,
or call toll-free 1-800-582-2665

First Edition
Printed in Hong Kong

Acknowledgments

A book of this kind would never reach publication without the generous assistance of many people. The curators and their assistants in the herbaria of several universities allowed the author to browse their collections in order to locate and identify many penstemons in the Northwest. Much appreciation is due the following: John Rumely and Cathy Siebert, Montana State University; David Dyer, University of Montana; Doug Henderson and Angela Sondenaa, University of Idaho; Joanna Schultz and Joy Mastrogiuseppe, Washington State University; and Kenton Chambers, Oregon State University. Jeanette Oliver, Flathead Valley Community College, assisted with the loan of equipment.

Others freely offered their knowledge of locations of some of the rarer species, including: Sherm Karl, Fort Keogh Livestock and Range Laboratory, Miles City, Montana, for *P. grandiflorus*; Joe Duft, Boise, Idaho, Roger Rosentreter, Boise, Bureau of Land Management, Michael Mancuso, Boise, and Pat Packard, Nampa, Idaho, for locations of the rarer ones in southern Idaho and southeastern Oregon, especially *Penstemon janishiae, seorsus* and *idahoensis*. Shirley Backman helped to locate *P. kingii* and *P. gracilentus* and Anne Spiegel gave directions for finding *P. compactus*. John Roden of Lima, Montana, allowed me to photograph *P. montanus* in his wildflower garden. Bonnie Heidel, Montana Natural Heritage Program, Helena, Montana, supplied useful literature and other helpful assistance. A grateful *thank you* goes to each of these nice people.

In the preparation of this book's Key to Northwest Penstemons the author relied heavily on keys by previous authors. The keys that proved most helpful were by Cronquist (Hitchcock et al. 1994), Holmgren, Lodewick, Abrams, Dorn and McGregor et al. Also, Robin Lodewick was most helpful by reviewing my key and offering suggestions. The descriptions of plants and their ranges by the above authors and by Keck (1932 to1945) were also invaluable to the development of this volume. However, this book's key, plant descriptions and range information are the sole responsibility of the author.

Finally, I wish to acknowledge the outstanding work of Zoe Strickler in the graphic design of this volume. Anne Morley, botanist, naturalist, illustrator and friend, Swan Lake, Montana, whose diligence and talent with the illustrations make this book much more complete, also deserves special recognition and thanks.

Introduction

Penstemon is the largest genus of flowering plants native to North America, with about 272 species. This total may vary slightly, because botanists do not always agree on what constitutes a species or a variety of a species. Counting all the recognized varieties of the different species, a total of about 386 native varieties are now recognized, plus 15 close relatives that were at one time classed as penstemons but have more recently been moved to other genera (Straw 1966).

Penstemon is just one genus in the large figwort or snapdragon family, the gorgeous Scrophulariaceae. Penstemons have been largely ignored by flower gardeners in the United States, but their inclusion in perennial gardens is increasing as gardeners learn about them and their special needs. (For example, overwatering and too much fertilizer can be detrimental to many penstemons.)

The many species of *Penstemon* range from Alaska to the Northwest Territories and south to Guatemala. Every state in the union except Hawaii has at least one native species. Most penstemons prefer the drier regions of the West with Utah claiming the most, 64 species.

Many species of *Penstemon* thrive on disturbed ground. Frequently they pioneer on roadside banks or on hardscrabble gravel, sand or even in cracks in rock cliffs. Virtually all species require good soil drainage. Thus penstemons often do well in xeriscape and rock gardens, and some even thrive in almost pure sand. Also, most species need full sunlight for at least part of the day to do well in garden settings.

The name *Penstemon* comes from the prefix *pen,* meaning "almost," and *stamen;* thus it means "almost a stamen," and refers to the sterile stamen, called a *staminode,* typical of the genus. In the past, some authors have mistakenly assumed that the word comes from *penta* meaning "five" or "fifth" plus *stamen,* again referring to the staminode. They often erroneously spelled it *Pentstemon.* By botanical convention the original spelling in the first publication to use the name is the one that must be followed. Mitchell first described the genus *Penstemon* in 1748.

At one time *Penstemon* was strongly recommended to be named the national flower of the United States. Since each state has an official flower, and none of them are penstemons, Congress did not see fit to adopt a national flower.

Generally, penstemons have little or no forage value for livestock or game animals. Range livestock may pass up some penstemons in preference for almost any other plants, but in some cases they feed heartily on penstemons, especially on dry rangeland where penstemons may be the only succulent green forage available. Deer sometimes will nip the tender tops from garden penstemons, but they seldom if ever eat the entire plants. Some species may be more palatable than others, but no research is known to have been done on that subject.

Penstemons are not widely known for medical uses, although some references note the occasional use of penstemons in poultices, for the treatment of cuts and burns, by Native Americans and early pioneers. No particular species is generally recognized for such uses.

This book presents at least one color photograph of each of the 80 species of *Penstemon* (including one close relative) that occur in the Pacific Northwest in the states of Washington, Oregon, Idaho and Montana. The photos are accompanied by technical descriptions and by line drawings that illustrate important distinguishing characteristics of each. (In a few cases the color photographs do not show true color, especially with lavender flowers. Color slide film is more sensitive to the red component in lavender flowers than it is to the blue component, and those flowers may appear pink in the photos.)

Also, a range map shows the approximate natural location of each species and its varieties. The maps cannot be considered precise, because species ranges can change over time and new populations are still being discovered. However, the maps represent the best known range for each species. Also, the Idaho Highway Department has seeded penstemons along many of the roads in that state as part of a highway beautification program. Two of those species have become naturalized and are included in this book. However, since others are known to have been seeded, penstemons along Idaho highways that cannot be identified as native to the state can be attributed to the highway department's seeding program.

A key to penstemons of the Northwest, based on botanical characteristics, is included on pages 10–23 for specialists and anyone else interested in precise identification. To use the key effectively, one must be able to see fine details of flower and plant parts. Thus, it is helpful to use at least a 10-power hand lens and probably a 6-inch ruler graduated in millimeters. A dissecting microscope also comes in handy, but that is the province of the professional and is not essential.

The drawing of a cross section of a penstemon flower shows the parts of the blossoms described in the following paragraphs. Also see the photograph of a penstemon flower in cross section on page 55. All penstemon flowers have tubular corollas, composed of fused petals that flare to five petal lobes at the open end. Almost all of our Northwest penstemons have two-lipped corollas with two petal lobes above and three below. The corolla base rests in a calyx cup composed of five sepals that are shorter than the corolla. The sepals are fused together at the base, forming the shallow cup. Some botanists therefore refer to the "calyx lobes" rather than the sepals.

Each penstemon flower typically possesses four fertile stamens and one nonfertile or sterile stamen, the staminode. The fertile stamens attach to the inner base of the corolla tube and mostly remain included inside the tube. They form two pairs: one pair, supported on shorter filaments, attaches to the tube on either side of the ovary, the second pair, on longer filaments, attaches to the bottom of the

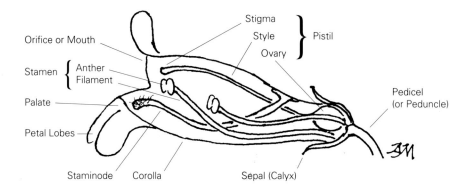

Orifice or Mouth

Stamen { Anther
Filament

Palate

Petal Lobes

Staminode   Corolla

Stigma
Style   } Pistil
Ovary

Pedicel
(or Peduncle)

Sepal (Calyx)

tube under the ovary. Very short, hairlike nectary glands are located at the base of the shorter filaments.

The staminode originates from the inner top surface (the "roof") of the corolla tube, ahead of the ovary, then drops down to the floor of the corolla, offering some protection to the ovary from invading insects. It may project out of (be *exserted* from) the throat of the tube or remain completely included within the tube. It may also wear a hairy "beard," a feature that gave rise to the common name "beard-tongue," or it may be smooth *(glabrous)*. In addition, the staminode may or may not be noticeably broadened or enlarged at the tip. Variations of these characteristics help in the identification of the various species.

The anthers, located on the ends of the stamens, produce pollen, and all have two pouches *(sacs)*. These attach to the ends of filaments as parallel pairs in the shape of horseshoes while in the buds and before they split open *(dehisce)* to release pollen. Their variation allows us to classify penstemons into subgenera. Some botanists have recognized as many as six subgenera of penstemons, with the huge subgenus *Penstemon* being further subdivided into ten sections. The key in this book recognizes four subgenera in the Pacific Northwest.

In the subgenus *Dasanthera,* for example, the anther sacs open flat to release pollen and wear dense coats of woolly hairs *(pubescence)* that generally obscure the outer surfaces. All the species in this subgenus occur in the Pacific Northwest and are subshrubs, mostly woody at the base and lower branches. A second sub-genus, *Saccanthera,* has anther sacs that remain permanently horseshoe-shaped and dehisce only at the inner ends and across the connective where the two sacs join, while the outer ends form permanent pouches or sacs. The third subgenus, *Habroanthus,* has anther sacs that dehisce only at the outer ends and remain closed at the inner ends across the connective. These sacs normally diverge (do not remain horseshoe-shaped) and the individual sacs may remain straight along the line of dehiscence in some species or they may twist so that the anthers become somewhat S-shaped in other species. Also, these anthers may be pubescent with short, scattered hairs in some species and glabrous in others. Finally, the fourth subgenus, *Penstemon,* has anther sacs that dehisce completely, even across the connective, and diverge at an angle from each other or spread opposite to each other. The key that follows provides descriptions defining various sections of the genus.

The pistil or female organ of a flower consists of the stigma, which collects pollen for fertilization, plus the style and the ovary. The stigma in penstemons is more or less enlarged *(capitate)* in comparison with the style, the stalk that connects it to the ovary, which is where the seeds develop. The style presses against the inner top of the corolla tube and often rests in a groove, seen as a ridge on top of the corolla of many species. The style bends down so that the stigma will receive pollen from insects when it is ready for pollination, but this happens only some hours after the blossom opens. Since pollinating insects more often than not enter the flower before the style bends, this helps to ensure cross-pollination and avoids self-fertilization.

The ovary is comprised of two chambers, called *carpels.* Each carpel has two sides and normally contains numerous seeds. In fruit the ovary expands into a dry teardrop-shaped capsule that eventually ruptures along the sutures joining the two carpels, and also often along sutures at the center lines of the carpels, to release the seeds.

When the corollas wither and fall off after pollination, they take the stamens with them, leaving the pistils with styles intact, still resting in the calyx cups. As the seeds ripen and the capsules expand, the styles wither and are usually cast off as well.

Penstemon is one native genus, among a relatively few others in the plant kingdom, that is still actively evolving. Thus, it is fairly easy to create new hybrids for the garden. New species or varieties are infrequently discovered in the wild. Hybridization in nature can cause considerable difficulty in identification of species. Sometimes the hybrid is fertile and can reproduce itself without both parent species being nearby. In other cases the hybrid may not be fertile and will only occur if the two parent species are within flying distance of specific pollinating insects or hummingbirds. The distances separating species into different ranges or habitats prevent a great deal more hybridization from occurring in nature. In general, hybridization of fertile species or varieties occurs most readily among closely related species, that is, within a subgenus or a section of a subgenus.

Penstemons are all perennials, some short-lived and others long-lived. The majority of species send up one to several stems in a clump from a branching, woody root crown, but some species form low mats of woody stems and leaves. Some species are evergreen. In most if not all species that produce basal leaf rosettes or sterile, nonflowering shoots at the base, some or all of the basal leaves remain green over winter. The majority of penstemon species are herbaceous, with the flowering stems dying back to the woody base or branches in winter. Furthermore, the *cauline* or flowering stems do not branch below the inflorescence in most species, but there are exceptions.

Some species, mainly in the subgenus *Dasanthera,* develop floral racemes in which each flower is supported by its individual pedicel that is attached directly to the main stem. A raceme in *Penstemon* usually has two flowers arising at each upper node in the axils of two opposite leaves or bracts. A more common inflorescence is a branching panicle in which two peduncles arise at each node and branch to support two or more blossoms each. Flowers in panicles always begin blooming from the bottom of the inflorescence upward. The individual branch of a panicle is often called a *cyme* or, more precisely, a *cymule*. Technically a cyme begins blooming with the terminal flower and progresses down the peduncle, but this is not a hard and fast rule in *Penstemon*.

When the nodes along the flowering stems are distinctly separate from each other vertically and three or more flowers cluster at the node, the false whorl that results is called a *verticillaster.* A verticillaster occurs where two peduncles (cymes) arise, each one in the axil of a leaf pair or opposite bracts. The peduncles may be very short or fairly long. If long, they may rise closely parallel to the stem and the flowers then appear as a tight cluster around the stem. On the other hand, some species of *Penstemon* display expanded inflorescences in which the fairly long peduncles spread away from the stem and branch widely, developing loose inflorescences. Finally, some species develop dense, rounded clusters of flowers, terminating the stem and also perhaps at the nodes, with indeterminate branching. Such a dense cluster of flowers is called a *thyrse.*

The leaves in *Penstemon* almost always occur in opposite pairs, except in four species, which are all present in the Pacific Northwest. *Penstemon triphyllus,* as the name implies, has some (but not all) leaves in whorls of three (or four) at the nodes. *Penstemon gairdneri,* on the other hand, has truly alternate leaves in the variety *gairdneri,* but one finds a mixture of mostly opposite and some alternate leaves in *Penstemon gairdneri* var. *oreganus.* The closely related *Penstemon seorsus* has mostly opposite leaves, but a few alternate or scattered leaves or bracts often appear in the upper inflorescence. *Penstemon deustus* var. *variabilis* can have whorls of three or four leaves per node as well as some opposite leaves and even a few scattered, alternate leaves, all on the same stem. A few scattered leaves may also occur at the top or bottom of the stem in *Penstemon cusickii* and *richardsonii.* All other penstemons normally only have opposite-paired leaves and floral bracts. As is true in most facets of life, however, aberrations can and often do occur. For botanists, Murphy's law holds that any specimen chosen for identification will be nontypical for the species. As an example, a picture of *Penstemon eriantherus* var. *whitedii* is shown on page 127 in which one blossom has six petal lobes and two staminodes.

Some penstemons have leaves only on the flowering stem (all cauline), although most of those leaves may be crowded near the base of the plant. Other species typically grow true rosettes of basal leaves and often develop sterile, nonflowering stems at the base that may or may not bear the largest leaves on the plant.

Four closely related genera of plants with four stamens and relatively large staminodes are *Chionophila, Keckiella, Nothochelone* and *Pennellianthus*. The flowers of all of these look much like *Penstemon* and all were included in the genus *Penstemon* at one time. Three of these genera differ from *Penstemon* by having nectar produced on disks that support the ovaries, whereas *Penstemon* species all produce nectar on unusual hairlike glands at the base of fertile stamens inside the corolla. The fourth genus, *Chionophila,* differs in the fruit and the calyx, among other features. *Pennellianthus frutescens* is the only species in its genus. It occurs in Japan and far eastern Siberia, but not in North America. *Nothochelone* has just one species and it is included in this book. *Chionophila* has two species, only one of which grows in the Northwest, in the Bitterroot Mountains of Montana and Idaho. *Keckiella* has several species, mostly in California, only one of which extends into the very southwestern corner of Oregon, *Keckiella lemmonii.*

If you find a *Penstemon* and want to identify the species, turn to the Key to Northwest Penstemons, page 10. It is a dichotomous key, designed to lead to one unique species or variety. At each point in the key you will have two options: one that describes the plant you wish to identify and one that does not. Follow the branch of the key that fits your specimen. At couplet 7 in the key, for example, 7a. applies only to flowers that are red or pink. If the flower that you want to identify is blue or purple, skip to 7b. and continue with couplet 9.

If any part of a description in the key is wrong for the flower in hand, reject that line of investigation and proceed with the other part of the couplet. If you are uncertain at some point as to which part of a couplet applies to your plant, check out both branches and look ahead at the couplets following either alternative. Then, when you can tentatively identity your species or variety, turn to the page with the detailed description, photograph and illustrations for that species to further conclude your identification. To help in your search, illustrations are liberally included to indicate features that may not show in the photographs. Always remember that penstemons sometimes hybridize and an identification can be a matter of which one comes closest to your specimen.

In some books the authors choose to use the term *subspecies* (ssp.) to denote variations within a species, while others use *variety* (var.). *Subspecies* and *variety* are considered here to be synonymous in *Penstemon* and I choose to use variety (var.) throughout.

In the key and descriptions of the species, many length measurements are given. Metric measurements appear first and are quite precise. Inches and fractions of inches may be given in parentheses and are less precise. With very small measurements the inch equivalents are usually deleted. On the last page a 15 cm (6 inch) ruler may prove helpful to some readers.

Key to Northwest Penstemons

1a. Anthers (pollen sacs) covered with long, tangled, woolly pubescence, generally obscuring the outer surfaces of the valves; corolla quite long, 25 to 40 mm (1–1¹/₂ in.), and keeled (ridged) on top; plants mostly shrubby (woody) at the base.
GROUP I. (subgenus *Dasanthera*) p. 10

1b. Anthers glabrous (smooth, nonhairy) or hairy-pubescent with sparse, generally short hairs (longer hairs in *P. caryi*) not obscuring the outer valve surfaces; corollas generally, but not always, smaller, 6 to 30 mm (¹/₄–1¹/₄ in.) long; plants mostly herbaceous or woody only at the ground.

2a. Anther sacs not dehiscing (opening) full length, remaining closed at least at one end.

3a. Anther sacs dehiscing in the middle, remaining closed at both ends (may open to, but not across, the connective). (*P. gracilis* and *P. euglaucus* sometimes have slightly pouched anthers.)

4a. Plants glabrous throughout; the inflorescence a densely clustered, globe-shaped, terminal thyrse, with or without 1 to 3 smaller verticillasters spaced lower on the stem; Blue Mts. of OR to cent ID and w MT.
78. *P. globosus* p. 178

4b. Plants glandular-hairy in the inflorescence, glabrous below; the inflorescence of 1 to several open or moderately dense verticillasters, the terminal cluster not densely globe-shaped; cent and s-cent ID to adj MT.
73. *P. attenuatus* var. *militaris* p. 168

3b. Anther sacs dehiscing at one end and remaining closed at the other.

5a. Anther sacs dehiscing across the connective joining the 2 sacs, but remaining closed at the outer end, forming terminal pouches; the sutures noticeably toothed; the sacs remaining permanently parallel or horseshoe-shaped. **GROUP II. (subgenus *Saccanthera*) p. 12**

5b. Anther sacs remaining closed at the inner ends (at the connective joining the 2 adjacent sacs), dehiscing at the outer ends of the sacs. (*P. payettensis* may open to the connective.)
GROUP III. (subgenus *Habroanthus*) p. 14

2b. Anther sacs dehiscing full length, including across the connective, the 2 sacs diverging or becoming opposite; anther sacs opening moderately to boat shape or completely flat (explanate). **GROUP IV. (subgenus *Penstemon*) p. 16**

Group I. Anthers Woolly-Pubescent
Subgenus *Dasanthera*

6a. Inflorescence glabrous (smooth); leaves bluish green from a glaucous coating, broad (width about ¹/₃ the length); endemic to the eastern end of the Columbia Gorge.
1. *P. barrettiae* p. 24

6b. Inflorescence densely to remotely glandular (with gland-tipped hairs); leaves mostly bright green (*P. rupicola* a glaucous exception), leaves variable in shape.

7a. Corolla rose red to pink.

    8a. Plants low, forming mats on rocky cliffs or outcrops; leaves blue-green glaucous; flowering stems 1 dm (4 in.) long or less; Cascade Mts., s WA to sw OR and n CA.
        2. *P. rupicola* p. 26

    8b. Plants erect or spreading, rarely mat-forming; leaves green; flowering stems 1 to 4 dm (4–16 in.) long; s Josephine Co., OR, and adj n CA.
        3. *P. newberryi* var. *berryi* p. 28

7b. Corolla blue to lavender or purple.

    9a. Inflorescence essentially a branching panicle.

        10a. Upper leaves linear to narrowly lanceolate, 3 to 10 mm (to ³/₈ in.) wide, finely toothed to entire; se BC, sw Alta., n ID and nw MT.   **4. *P. lyallii* p. 30**

        10b. Upper leaves broader, lanceolate to ovate, mostly 1¹/₂ to 4 cm (⁵/₈–1¹/₂ in.) wide; conspicuously toothed; Cascade and Coast Ranges.
        5. *Nothochelone nemorosa* p. 32

    9b. Inflorescence essentially a raceme, two flowers at each node on individual pedicels; plants generally low, mat-forming or not, 1 to 3 (max. 4) dm (4–12 in.) high.

        11a. Leaves all cauline (on the flowering stem) or occasionally on sterile stems subequal to the flowering stems in length; lower leaves smaller than the upper, not forming a basal cluster; cent ID to s-cent MT, w WY and cent UT.
        6. *P. montanus* p. 34

            A1. Leaves entire or mostly entire, glaucous, glabrous or pubescent, but not glandular.   **P. *montanus* var. *idahoensis***

            A2. Leaves markedly toothed, green, pubescent and usually glandular.
        P. *montanus* var. *montanus*

        11b. Leaves generally forming rosettes or mats, glabrous, basal leaves robust.

            12a. Leaves of the flowering stem well developed, generally larger than the basal leaves, elliptical and not sharp-pointed; plants often forming mats; n Rocky Mts.   **7. *P. ellipticus* p. 36**

            12b. Leaves of the flowering stem much reduced.

                13a. Flowering stems 1 dm (4 in.) high or less; plants mostly forming low, spreading mats; n coast of BC through Coast and Cascade ranges to the Sierras of CA, also in the Steens Mts. of se OR.
        8. *P. davidsonii* p. 38

                    A1. Corolla 3.4 to 4.5 cm (1¹/₄–1³/₄ in.) long; leaf tips sharp; Steens Mtn., OR.   **P. *davidsonii* var. *praeteritus***

                    A2. Corolla 2 to 3.6 cm (³/₄–1³/₈ in.) long; leaves mostly rounded or blunt.

                        B1. Leaves entire, spatulate or broadest near the end and consistently rounded; s WA Cascades to Sierras of CA.
        P. *davidsonii* var. *davidsonii*

B2. Leaves markedly or remotely serrate, lanceolate and broadest below the middle; s Vancouver Is., Olympic Mts. and n Cascades in WA.
P. davidsonii var. menziesii

13b. Flowering stems generally 2 to 4 dm (8–16 in.) high; plants spreading or not.

14a. Cauline leaves mostly acute, serrate or entire; the inflorescence usually tightly secund (on one side of the stem); e of the Cascade Crest, s BC to w MT, w WY and cent OR. **9. P. fruticosus p. 40**

A1. Leaf blades mostly 1 to 2½ cm (to 1 in.) long and sharply toothed (dentate); w-cent ID, se WA and ne OR. **P. fruticosus var. serratus**

A2. Leaves generally longer and entire or finely toothed.

B1. Leaves linear or very narrow, mostly 6 to 10 times as long as wide, the blades 2 to 5 cm (to 2 in.) long; n ID, ne WA and se BC.
P. fruticosus var. scouleri

B2. Leaves broader, usually 2 to 7 times as long as wide, the blade to 6 cm (2+ in.) long; s BC e of the Cascade Crest to MT, WY and cent OR, except in the ranges of the other 2 varieties.
P. fruticosus var. fruticosus

14b. Cauline leaves rounded or obtuse, entire or minutely serrate.

15a. Some inflorescences with 4 to 8 verticillasters, tightly secund; generally lavender, also reported as pink; s Josephine Co., OR, and adj n CA.
3. P. newberryi var. berryi p. 28

15b. Inflorescences commonly with 1 to 3 verticillasters, tending to spread; usually purplish; w of the Cascade Crest, sw WA to the Coast Range in OR.
10. P. cardwellii p. 42

Group II. Anther Sacs Parallel or Horseshoe-shaped
Subgenus *Saccanthera*
(*P. gracilis* and *P. euglaucus* occasionally have slightly pouched sacs)

16a. Plants covered with glandular hairs throughout; plants herbaceous, woody only at the ground line; basal leaves large. **11. P. glandulosus p. 44**

A1. Leaves serrate; Blue Mts., se WA, ne OR, and adjacent ID.
P. glandulosus var. glandulosus

A2. Leaves entire; e slope of the Cascade Mts., Chelan Co., WA, to Hood River Co., OR. **P. glandulosus var. chelanensis**

16b. Plants glabrous or with short, non-glandular pubescence on stems and leaves below the inflorescence, glabrous or glandular in the inflorescence; plants woody (subshrubs) at the base; basal leaves on sterile shoots often lacking (3 exceptions: *P. roezlii, laetus* and *leonardii*).

17a. Leaves toothed on the margins.

18a. Plants glandular in the inflorescence.

19a. Some leaves whorled in 3s or 4s at the nodes (some leaves may be opposite or somewhat scattered on the stem); Snake River Canyon and lower reaches of tributaries, ID, OR and WA to the Columbia River below Snake River. **12. *P. triphyllus* p. 46**

19b. Leaves in opposite pairs (may be occasionally offset, i.e. subopposite).

20a. Leaves deeply and sharply toothed (dentate), $^1/_5$ or more of the way to the midrib; corolla generally more than 20 mm ($^3/_4$ in.) long (*P. richardsonii* var. *curtiflorus* in n-cent OR, 15 to 20 mm [$^5/_8$–$^3/_4$ in.] long); the Columbia Basin e of the Cascade Crest.   **13. *P. richardsonii* p. 48**

A1. Corolla 15 to 20 mm ($^5/_8$–$^3/_4$ in.) long; staminode not bearded; n-cent OR (Wheeler and Wasco Cos.).
P. richardsonii* var. *curtiflorus

A2. Corolla 22 to 32 mm ($^7/_8$–$1^1/_4$ in.) long; staminode bearded.

B1. Leaves narrow and deeply and irregularly dentate about halfway to the midrib; s BC to n OR in the Columbia Basin.
P. richardsonii* var. *richardsonii

B2. Leaves mostly ovate, shallowly and regularly toothed, the upper surfaces gray-pubescent; n-cent OR (Wasco to Grant and Union Cos.) ***P. richardsonii* var. *dentatus***

20b. Leaves shallowly toothed (serrate); corolla 12 to 19 mm ($^1/_2$–$^3/_4$ in.) long; Bitterroot Mts. of MT and ID, disjunct in se WA.   **14. *P. diphyllus* p. 50**

18b. Plants essentially glabrous throughout, except for minute pubescence on peduncles in *P. serrulatus*.

21a. Stamen filaments glabrous below the anther sacs; corolla 15 to 25 mm ($^5/_8$–1 in.) long; Cascades to the Coast.   **15. *P. serrulatus* p. 52**

21b. Filaments pubescent just below the sacs (unique among all penstemons in this regard); corolla 25 to 38 mm (1–$1^1/_2$ in.) long; Blue Mts. of OR and WA and adj ID.   **16. *P. venustus* p. 54**

17b. Leaves essentially entire on the margins.

22a. Plants glandular in the inflorescence; glabrous below or with short, non-glandular hairs on the lower stems and leaves.

23a. Staminode bearded; leaves mostly near the base of the plant, widely spaced above; mountains of Lake Co., OR, to n NV and ne CA.
17. *P. gracilentus* p. 56

23b. Staminode glabrous; flower stem leafy.

24a. Herbage densely gray-pubescent; stems decumbent (curved) at the base; basal leaves lacking; anther sacs 1 to $1^1/_2$ mm long; Great Basin, s Malheur Co., OR, and much of NV.   **18. *P. kingii* p. 58**

24b. Herbage green, remotely pubescent; stems ascending; basal leaves on sterile shoots; anther sacs $1^1/_2$ to 2 mm long; cent to sw OR to NV and CA.

25a. Corolla 14 to 20 mm ($^1/_2$–$^3/_4$ in.) long; anthers broadly rounded at the connective and stubby; cent and sw OR to NV and CA.   **19. *P. roezlii* p. 60**

25b. Corolla 2 to 3 cm ($^3/_4$–1$^3/_{16}$ in.) long; anthers sagittate (arrow-shaped, narrow at the connective), elongate; sw OR (Josephine, Jackson and Klamath Cos.) and n CA.   **20. *P. laetus* var. *sagittatus* p. 62**

22b. Plants glabrous throughout or with short, non-glandular hairs on the upper stem.

26a. Leaves linear, approximately 10 times as long as wide; e OR and sw ID.   **21. *P. cusickii* p. 64**

26b. Leaves broader, approximately 2 to 5 times as long as wide.

27a. Herbage green; leaves narrowly oblong to oblanceolate, approximately 5 times as long as wide; Bear River Mts., se ID and n UT, disjunct in sw UT.   **22. *P. leonardii* p.66**

27b. Herbage blue-green glaucous; upper leaves wider, approximately 2 to 4 times as long as wide; sw OR, Siskiyou Mts. to n CA.

28a. Corolla 2 to 3 cm ($^3/_4$–1$^3/_{16}$ in.) long; stems 2 to 5 dm (8–20 in.) tall; inflorescence a raceme; sw OR and nw CA.   **23. *P. azureus* p. 68**

28b. Corolla 1.4 to 2 cm ($^1/_2$–$^3/_4$ in.) long; stems 1$^1/_2$ to 3 dm (6–12 in.) tall; inflorescence in part a branching panicle.   **24. *P. parvulus* p. 70**

Group III. Anther Sacs Dehiscing on the Outer Ends
Subgenus *Habroanthus*

29a. Corolla scarlet; tube spreading very moderately; exotic species native to sw US, seeded along highways in s ID by the Idaho Highway Dept. and now naturalized. (3 varieties, most commonly var. *undosus*).   **25. *P. eatonii* p. 72**

29b. Corolla blue to violet or purple.

30a. Anther sacs with long flexuous, non-dense pubescence, equal in length to the width of the sacs or more.

31a. Leaves and stems surface-glandular, commonly bearing adhered, glistening soil particles; leaves linear-oblanceolate and 5 to 10 times as long as wide; anther sacs dehiscing by a narrow slot; s-cent ID (Cassia Co.) to ne NV and nw UT.   **26. *P. idahoensis* p. 74**

31b. Leaves and stems glabrous; leaves linear, 15 to 25 times as long as wide; anther sacs boat-shaped; Pryor and Bighorn Mts., s-cent MT and n-cent WY.   **27. *P. caryi* p. 76**

30b. Anther sacs with short, stiff, scattered pubescence or glabrous; leaves variable.

32a. Anthers glabrous, except for minute hairs or teeth on the sutures.

33a. Anther sacs essentially straight (not curved or twisted); leaves mostly broad, 1$^1/_2$ to 5 cm ($^1/_2$–2 in.) wide, lanceolate to ovate; upper leaves usually about twice as long as wide; se Blue Mts. of OR to w MT.   **28. *P. payettensis* p. 78**

33b. Anther sacs curved or twisted so the anthers appear S-shaped; leaves narrower, $^1/_2$ to 2 cm ($^1/_4$–$^3/_4$ in.) wide; upper leaves mostly $3^1/_2$ to 10 times as long as wide.

    34a. Corolla 18 to 22 mm ($^3/_4$–$^7/_8$ in.) long; staminode bearded; sepals 3 to 5 mm (to $^3/_{16}$ in.) long; Snake River Plain of s ID. **29. *P. perpulcher* p. 80**

    34b. Corolla 25 to 35 mm (1–1$^3/_8$ in.) long; staminode glabrous; sepals 5 to 10 mm (to $^3/_8$ in.) long; cent WA to sw ID and n UT to sw OR and s CA. **30. *P. speciosus* p. 82**

32b. Anthers pubescent with straight, stiff hairs (only at the connective in *P. pennellianus*).

    35a. Stem leaves narrow to linear, 5 to 10 (max.15) mm ($^3/_{16}$–$^5/_8$ in.) wide, length variable.

        36a. Staminode glabrous; anther sacs twisted or curved; sepals 7 to 11 mm (to $^7/_{16}$ in.) long; e-cent ID and sw MT. **31. *P. lemhiensis* p. 84**

        36b. Staminode bearded; anther sacs variable; sepals 4 to 7 mm long.

            37a. Inflorescence glandular; se ID, sw WY and n UT. **32. *P. subglaber* p. 86**

            37b. Inflorescence glabrous; se ID, w WY and ne UT. **35. *P. cyananthus* var. *subglaber* p. 92**

    35b. Stem leaves broader, lanceolate to ovate.

        38a. Anther sacs dehiscing $^4/_5$ of their length or more, some opening to but not across the connective; se MT and ne to cent WY. **33. *P. glaber* var. *glaber* p. 88**

        38b. Anther sacs dehiscing no more than $^4/_5$ of their length.

            39a. Anther sacs remaining essentially straight after dehiscing, the line of the sutures not curved to one side.

                40a. Plants dwarfed, compact, generally 1 to 2 dm (4–8 in.) high; sepals glandular; inflorescence dense and secund (all on one side of the stem), of 2 or 3 verticillasters; Bear River Mts., se ID to cent UT. **34. *P. compactus* p. 90**

                40b. Plants taller, generally 2 to 7 dm (8–28 in.) tall; sepals glabrous; inflorescence of 2 to 5 well-separated verticillasters, mostly to entirely encircling the stem; se ID to w WY and ne UT and possibly sw MT. **35. *P. cyananthus* var. *cyananthus* p. 92**

            39b. Anther sacs curved, the anthers somewhat S-shaped.

                41a. Sepals ovate to nearly round (as wide as long) and erose (raggedly toothed on the margins); Snake River Plain, s ID to sw MT. **36. *P. cyaneus* p. 94**

                41b. Sepals narrow and acuminate (curved inward to a sharp point); n Blue Mts., se WA and n Wallowa Co., OR. **37. *P. pennellianus* p. 96**

Group IV. Anthers Dehiscing Full Length, Usually Across the Connective
Subgenus *Penstemon*, mostly

42a. Plants shrubby (woody) at the base and lower branches; leaves toothed and leathery; corolla white or pale yellow, sometimes with red guide lines; corolla may be glandular within; cent WA to sw MT, nw WY and s CA. **38. *P. deustus* p. 98**

    A1. Some leaves 3- or 4-whorled at the nodes, leaves entire or minutely serrate near the tips; n-cent OR into s-cent WA in Klickitat Co. ***P. deustus* var. *variabilis***

    A2. Leaves all opposite, markedly toothed throughout.

        B1. Corolla less than 1 cm (³/₈ in.) long; staminode bearded; sw OR and nw CA. ***P. deustus* var. *suffrutescens***

        B2. Corolla more than 1 cm long; staminode glabrous.

            C1. Corolla 12 to18 mm (to ¹¹/₁₆ in.) long, the upper petal lobes white or cream-colored; cent WA, ne OR, ID, sw MT and nw WY. ***P. deustus* var. *deustus***

            C2. Corolla generally smaller, 10 to 15 mm (to ⁹/₁₆ in.) long, the upper petal lobes brownish; se OR and sw ID to n NV and ne CA. ***P. deustus* var. *pedicellatus***

42b. Plants herbaceous, woody only at the very base; leaves and corolla variable.

    43a. Leaves linear, 2 (max. 3) mm wide or less.

        44a. Leaves needle-shaped, about 1 mm wide, forming a dense tuft or rosette at the base; all cauline leaves in opposite pairs, not revolute.

            45a. Anther sacs narrowly dehiscent, oblong; inflorescence glabrous; corolla pink to lavender; sepals 4 to 6 mm (to ¹/₄ in.) long with acuminate tips; Pryor Mts. area of s-cent MT into WY. **39. *P. laricifolius* var. *laricifolius* p. 100**

            45b. Anther sacs ovate to rotund; inflorescence glandular; corolla blue-purple; sepals 2¹/₂ to 4 mm long, ovate to rotund with a short tip; sw MT, se ID and n-cent WY. **40. *P. aridus* p. 102**

        44b. Leaves, some or all, 2 mm wide, some on sterile shoots, but not forming a dense basal tuft; some leaves alternate or scattered on the stem and mostly revolute.

            46a. Leaf bases connected, clasping or making a ridge around the stem, some may be offset and not quite opposite near the top of the stem; corolla glabrous and white within; corolla lobes approximately ¹/₄ the length of the corolla tube; cent OR to sw ID. **41. *P. seorsus* p. 104**

            46b. Leaf bases separate, leaves alternate or some leaves scattered on the stem (leaves of *P. gairdneri* var. *oreganus* may all be opposite); corolla glandular within the throat and on the palate; corolla lobes larger, approximately ¹/₃ the tube length; cent WA and cent OR to Valley Co., ID. **42. *P. gairdneri* p. 106**

A1. Leaves alternate (may be a few opposite); cent WA to cent and
e-cent OR. ***P. gairdneri* var. *gairdneri***

A2. Leaves opposite, usually with a few scattered or alternate leaves on the
stem; Union and Baker Cos., OR, to Valley Co., ID.

P. gairdneri* var. *oreganus

43b. Leaves broader, more than 3 mm ($^1/_8$ in.) wide.

47a. Plants entirely herbaceous above ground, stems single or branching from the
root crown below ground; leaves toothed slightly or all entire; corolla pale violet,
nearly white within and marked with guide lines in the throat; e MT and WY and
the Great Plains. **43. *P. gracilis* p. 108**

47b. Plants woody at the ground line; not as described above.

48a. Corolla white or creamy with glandular pubescence within; e MT and the
Great Plains. **44. *P. albidus* p. 110**

48b. Corolla pink, blue or purple, sometimes pubescent within, but not white
or cream-colored.

49a. Some stem leaves connate-perfoliate (leaf pairs joined at the base
around the stem); corolla 27 to 35 mm (1+ in.) long; an alien species
seeded along ID highways (3 varieties may occur).

45. *P. palmeri* p. 112

49b. Leaves not connate-perfoliate; native species.

50a. Corolla large, 35 to 50 mm ($1^3/_8$–2 in.) long; plant glabrous
throughout; staminode included within the corolla; e MT and the
Great Plains. **46. *P. grandiflorus* p. 114**

50b. Corolla smaller, 25 mm (1 in.) long or less.

51a. Anther valves on mature flowers dehiscing narrowly to
oblong slots or very narrow boat shape (observe several).

52a. Leaves markedly dentate, ash-colored and densely
short-hairy; stems mostly 3 to 4 dm (12–16 in.) tall;
n-cent OR in the Deschutes and John Day river
drainages. **52. *P. eriantherus* var. *argillosus* p. 126**

52b. Leaves entire; not as described above.

53a. Stem short, 8 to 18 cm (3–7 in.) tall; guide lines
prominent in the throat; cent WY to nw CO and
UT, reported in sw MT. **47. *P. arenicola* p. 116**

53b. Stems longer, generally 2 to 6 dm (8–24 in.) tall;
guide lines absent or not.

54a. Leafy bracts in the inflorescence wider than
long, fleshy; cent WA to n-cent OR; se OR
and sw ID to nw NV.

48. *P. acuminatus* p. 118

A1. Corolla 10 to 15 mm ($^3/_8$–$^5/_8$ in.) long; calyx $4^1/_2$ to $6^1/_2$ mm long; s-cent OR, sw ID and nw NV. *P. acuminatus* var. *latebracteatus*

A2. Corolla 15 to 20 mm ($^5/_8$–$^3/_4$ in.) long; calyx 5 to 11 mm long; Columbia Basin, s-cent WA and n-cent OR. *P. acuminatus* var. *acuminatus*

54b. Bracts narrower, longer than broad.

55a. Floral bracts many times longer than broad, acute or acuminate, fleshy, glaucous; e MT and the Dakotas to n NM, ne AZ and cent UT.
49. *P. angustifolius* var. *angustifolius* p. 120

55b. Bracts of the lower inflorescence broadly lanceolate, ovate or rotund, $1^1/_2$ to 2 (max. 3) times as long as wide.

56a. Bearded portion of the staminode elongated, not tufted, the hairs normally well over $^1/_2$ mm long; w MT to the Great Plains, s Alta. to Man. and n WY. **50. *P. nitidus* p. 122**

A1. Leaves and bracts of the lower inflorescence broadly ovate to nearly round; calyx 3 to 6 mm (to $^1/_4$ in.) long.
P. nitidus var. *nitidus*

A2. Leaves and bracts of the inflorescence narrowly lanceolate, much longer than broad; calyx 5 to 8 mm (to $^5/_{16}$ in.) long.
P. nitidus var. *polyphyllus*

56b. Bearded portion of the staminode tufted, the hairs about $^1/_2$ mm long or the staminode glabrous; central WA to n-cent OR and se OR, sw ID to nw NV. **48. *P. acuminatus* var. *acuminatus* p. 118**

51b. Anther valves dehiscing to moderately broad boat shape or explanate (completely flat).

57a. Leaves mostly (or some) toothed on the margins (some leaves occasionally toothed in *P. attenuatus* and *P. rydbergii*); inflorescence glandular, rather open and few-flowered; corolla typically pale in the throat and marked with guide lines.
GROUP IV-A. (mostly section *Humiles*) p. 18

57b. Leaves entire (occasional exceptions noted above); inflorescence glabrous or glandular, generally tightly crowded with many flowers in one or more verticillasters or thyrses (*P. aridus* an exception); corolla not usually pale in the throat or marked with guide lines. **GROUP IV-B. (mostly section *Proceri*) p. 20**

**Group IV-A. Anthers Dehiscing Completely;
Leaves Toothed, Some Remotely; Inflorescence Glandular**
Section *Humiles*, mostly

58a. Stems short, 1 to 3 dm (4–12 in.), rarely to 4 dm (16 in.).

59a. Staminode exserted well beyond the corolla throat and with prominent orange beard.

60a. Corolla deeply incised on the sides into two lips; leaves entire or toothed only at the apex; sw ID, se OR, n NV and ne CA. **51. *P. janishiae* p. 124**

60b. Corolla 2-lipped, but not deeply incised on the sides; leaves toothed, sometimes remotely; se BC to ND, WY, cent OR and cent ID.
52. *P. eriantherus* p. 126

A1. Anther sacs mostly explanate (flat) and broad, approximately as long as broad with long lines of contact between the 2 halves; ne WA, se BC and s Alta., most of MT and e to cent ND, nw NE and n-cent CO.
P. eriantherus* var. *eriantherus

A2. Anther sacs mostly boat-shaped and oval, 1¹/₂ to 2¹/₂ times as long as broad with a relatively short line of contact.

B1. Upper stem leaves sessile, 5 to 10 times as long as broad; calyx 4 to 6 mm (to ¹/₄ in.) long; sw MT and cent ID to Baker and Union Cos., OR. ***P. eriantherus* var. *redactus***

B2. Upper stem leaves cordate clasping, 3 to 4 times as long as broad; calyx 7 to 12 mm (to ¹/₂ in.) long; cent WA, Chelan and Douglas Cos. ***P. eriantherus* var. *whitedii***

59b. Staminode included or reaching the orifice with yellow beard or glabrous.

61a. Corolla small, 11 to 16 mm (⁷/₁₆–⁵/₈ in.) long; e slope of the Cascades into the Columbia Basin in cent WA and s BC. **53. *P. pruinosus* p. 128**

61b. Corolla larger, 15 to 24 mm (⁵/₈–1 in.) long.

62a. Leaves bright green, lightly or remotely toothed; stems glabrous, mostly less than 3 dm (12 in.) tall.

63a. Stem leaves lightly short-hairy; ridge tops and upper slopes above Hell's Canyon, OR and ID. **54. *P. elegantulus* p. 130**

63b. Stem leaves glabrous; se BC and sw Alta. to w MT and s ID.
55. *P. albertinus* p. 132

62b. Leaves ash-colored, densely short-hairy and dentate; stems retrorsely (pointed downward) pubescent with short, stiff hairs, mostly 3 to 4 dm (12–16 in.) tall; n-cent OR in the Deschutes and John Day river drainages. **52. *P. eriantherus* var. *argillosus* p. 126**

58b. Stems generally longer, mostly 4 to 10 dm (16–40 in.) long.

64a. Sepals 5 to 11 mm (³/₁₆–³/₈ in.) long, narrow and green, not scarious (white) on the margins.

65a. Corolla 13 to 18 mm (¹/₂–³/₄ in.) long; sw OR and n CA.
56. *P. anguineus* p. 134

65b. Corolla 18 to 30 mm (³/₄–1¹/₈ in.) long.

66a. Lower lip much longer than the upper; staminode well exserted.

67a. Calyx 2 to 6 mm long; staminode glabrous or bearded with a tuft at the end; sw MT, se ID to se WY, CO, AZ and UT.
57. *P. whippleanus* p. 136

67b. Calyx 6 to 9 mm (to $^3/_8$ in.) long; staminode bearded $^1/_2$ length or more; Coast Range and s Willamette Valley, sw OR and nw CA.

58. *P. rattanii* var. *rattanii* p. 138

66b. Lower lip subequal to the upper; staminode included; n-cent OR in the Deschutes and John Day river drainages.

52. *P. eriantherus* var. *argillosus* p. 126

64b. Sepals 3 to 5 mm ($^1/_8$–$^3/_{16}$ in.) long and generally scarious-margined.

68a. Inflorescence expanded; cymes often long and many-flowered (10 to 20); corolla 15 to 23 mm ($^5/_8$–$^{15}/_{16}$ in.) long.

69a. Leaves coarse-toothed and finely pubescent; inflorescence strongly glandular; s BC to n OR, w of the Cascade Crest.   **59. *P. ovatus* p. 140**

69b. Leaves fine-toothed and usually glabrous; inflorescence lightly to moderately glandular; n ID and w MT to e WA, ne OR and cent ID.

60. *P. wilcoxii* p. 142

68b. Inflorescence narrow and few-flowered (2 to 6 blossoms per cyme); corolla generally smaller, 12 to 16 mm ($^1/_2$–$^5/_8$ in.) long.

70a. Cymes usually 1- to 4-flowered; e slope of the Cascades, WA to Mt. Hood, OR.   **61. *P. subserratus* p. 144**

70b. Cymes usually 4- to 6-flowered; generally nw MT to Lemhi Co., ID.

55. x 60. *P. wilcoxii* x *albertinus* (hybrid) p. 142

Group IV-B. Leaves Entire; Inflorescence Glabrous or Glandular
Section *Proceri*

71a. Corolla white, cream, pale pink or yellow. (*P. peckii, procerus* and *washingtonensis* may develop pink corollas).

72a. Corolla 4 to 12 mm ($^3/_{16}$–$^1/_2$ in.) long; anther sacs about $^1/_2$ mm long; staminode tip not expanded; se BC, sw Alta., w MT to ne OR.   **62. *P. confertus* p. 146**

72b. Corolla 11 to 16+ mm ($^3/_8$–$^5/_8$ in.) long; anther sacs $^1/_2$ to 1 mm long; staminode tip noticeably expanded.

73a. Corolla white or cream (may be intermixed with pink and blue in hybrid swarms); calyx mostly entire; se OR, sw ID and adj n NV.

63. *P. pratensis* p. 148

73b. Corolla yellow or pink; calyx erose-toothed on the margins.

74a. Staminode well included within the corolla; plants spreading by rhizomes and often mat-forming; corolla bright yellow; Bitterroot Mts., w MT and e-cent ID.   **64. *P. flavescens* p. 150**

74b. Staminode reaching the orifice or exserted; plants not mat-forming; corolla pale yellow or pink; sw WA and adj n ID. Often in hybrid swarms.   **73. *P. attenuatus* var. *attenuatus* p. 168**

71b. Corolla blue or purple.

75a. Inflorescence glandular.

76a. Plants forming mats; stems often pubescent in lines; alpine endemic to Wallowa Mts., ne OR. **65. *P. spatulatus* p. 152**

76b. Plants not as described above.

    77a. Leaves all cauline, not forming basal rosettes or sterile basal shoots.

        78a. Corolla 16 to 23 mm ($^5/_8$–$^7/_8$ in.) long; corolla white inside with blue or purple guide lines on the palate; sw MT and e ID to n NV and CO. **66. *P. radicosus* p. 154**

        78b. Corolla very small, 8 to 10 mm ($^3/_8$ in. or less) long; pale blue inside without noticeable guide lines; e base of the Cascades in Deschutes Co., OR. **67. *P. peckii* p. 156**

    77b. Some leaves forming basal rosettes or plants with leafy, sterile shoots at the base.

        79a. Stems short, generally 1 to 3 dm (4–12 in.) long.

            80a. Leaves glabrous except for the margins on some plants.

                81a. Calyx lobes broad with a short, sharp tip; se ID to sw MT and n-cent WY. **40. *P. aridus* p. 102**

                81b. Calyx lobes lanceolate, tapering to the tip; endemic to Chelan and Okanogan Cos., WA, in the higher mountains. **68. *P. washingtonensis* p. 158**

            80b. Leaves densely short-hairy.

                82a. Corolla 16 to 22 mm ($^5/_8$–$^7/_8$ in.) long; anther sacs about $^1/_2$ to just over 1 mm long.

                    83a. Anther sacs dehiscing broadly to explanate; leaves lanceolate, 4 to 12 mm (to $^1/_2$ in.) wide, entire or toothed.

                        84a. Staminode long exserted, tip curled under; corolla deeply incised on the sides so lips are nearly $^1/_2$ the corolla length; sw ID, s Harney Co., OR, NV and ne CA. **51. *P. janishiae* p. 124**

                        84b. Staminode barely exserted, tip straight; corolla 2-lipped, but not deeply incised on the sides, lip less than $^1/_3$ the corolla length; se OR, sw ID to cent NV and ne CA. **69. *P. miser* p. 160**

                    83b. Anther sacs boat-shaped; leaves linear, 1 to 2.5 mm wide, entire; endemic to se ID. **70. *P. pumilus* p. 162**

                82b. Corolla 12 to 16 mm ($^1/_2$–$^5/_8$ in.) long; anther sacs about $^1/_2$ mm long; cent WA to cent ID, w CO and e CA. **71. *P. humilis* var. *humilis* p. 164**

        79b. Stems generally longer, 3 dm (12 in.) long or more.

85a. Corolla very small, 8 to 10 mm (to ³/₈ in.) or less long; anther sacs about ¹/₂ mm long; leaves almost all cauline; e base of the Cascades in Deschutes Co., OR. **67. *P. peckii* p. 156**

85b. Corolla larger, 12 to 20 mm (¹/₂–³/₄ in.) long; basal leaves well developed.

86a. Leaves glaucous; leaf tips rounded; upper leaves much reduced, narrow to linear; staminode not expanded at the tip; Lake Co., OR, local endemic. **72. *P. glaucinus* p. 166**

86b. Leaves green; leaf tips acute; upper leaves robust; staminode noticeably expanded at the tip; cent WA to w MT, s ID and n-cent WY. **73. *P. attenuatus* p. 168**

A1. Anther sacs not dehiscing full length, often to, but not across the connective and not reaching the free tips; s ID. ***P. attenuatus* var. *militaris***

A2. Anther sacs dehiscing completely, but not spreading flat (explanate).

B1. Corolla 7 to 12 mm (to ¹/₂ in.) long; wet meadows in the s Blue Mts., OR. ***P. attenuatus* var. *palustris***

B2. Corolla normally longer than 12 mm long; habitat variable and ranges as shown on p. 168.

C1. Stems generally short, 2 to 3¹/₂ dm (8–14 in.) tall; sepals oval and broadly scarious; corolla blue-purple; se ID, sw MT and nw WY. ***P. attenuatus* var. *pseudoprocerus***

C2. Stems taller, 3 to 9 dm (12–36 in.); sepals lanceolate and narrowly scarious; corolla blue-purple, pinkish or yellow; e WA and ne OR to w MT and sw ID. ***P. attenuatus* var. *attenuatus***

75b. Inflorescence glabrous or pubescent with short, non-glandular hairs.

87a. Corolla very small, 5 to 10 mm (³/₁₆–³/₈ in.) long.

88a. Inflorescence densely crowded at the apex, composed of many flowers, some declined (angled downward) on the underside of the thyrse(s); basal leaves usually present; leaves lanceolate to ovate, mostly straight, not arched; widespread species, AK and the Yukon to CA and CO. **74. *P. procerus* p. 170**

A1. Plants dwarf, mostly ¹/₂ to 1¹/₂ dm (2–6 in.) tall, usually with 1 dense thyrse at the apex, occasionally with 1 or 2 verticillasters; alpine and subalpine.

B1. Calyx 3 to 6 mm (to ¹/₄ in.) high, the sepals caudate-tipped or narrow and acute; Olympic and Cascade Mts. of WA and BC. ***P. procerus* var. *tolmiei***

B2. Calyx 1¹/₂ to 3 mm (to ¹/₈ in.) high, the sepals rounded or truncate, often with a short sharp tip; Wallowa Mts., OR to NV and CA. ***P. procerus* var. *formosus***

A2. Plants larger, mostly 1$\frac{1}{2}$ to 3 dm (6–12 in.) tall, usually with 2 to 4 verticillasters in the inflorescence.

C1. Calyx 3 to 6 mm (to $\frac{1}{4}$ in.) high, the sepals caudate-tipped or narrow and acute; AK and the Yukon to the e base of the Cascades in WA, to ne OR, MT and CO. **P. procerus var. procerus**

C2. Calyx 1$\frac{1}{2}$ to 3 mm (to $\frac{1}{8}$ in.) high, the sepals rounded or truncate, often with a short, sharp tip; Wallowa Mts., OR, OR Cascades to n CA. **P. procerus var. brachyanthus**

88b. Inflorescence few-flowered at the apex and more open, flowers inclined upward or horizontal; basal leaves lacking; leaves narrow to linear, arching and recurved; e base of the Cascades, cent OR to n CA. **75. P. cinicola p. 172**

87b. Corolla larger, 11 to 20 mm ($\frac{3}{8}$–$\frac{13}{16}$ in.) long.

89a. Leaves all cauline (on the stem).

90a. Corolla narrowly tubular, not much expanded at the throat, 2 to 3 mm (to $\frac{1}{8}$ in.) wide when pressed; palate densely bearded, completely filling the throat; s ID, n of Snake River Plain. **76. P. laxus p. 174**

90b. Corolla spreading, 3 to 6 mm (to $\frac{1}{4}$ in.) wide at the throat; palate moderately bearded; s ID, s of Snake River Plain, NV and UT. **77. P. watsonii p. 176**

89b. Basal rosette of leaves well developed, many on sterile, nonflowering shoots.

91a. Corolla relatively large, 15 to 20 mm ($\frac{5}{8}$–$\frac{13}{16}$ in.) long; inflorescence a dense, globe-shaped terminal thyrse, may develop 1 or 2 crowded verticillasters below the apex; Blue Mts. of ne OR to cent ID and w MT. **78. P. globosus p. 178**

91b. Corolla smaller, generally 11 to 15 mm ($\frac{3}{8}$–$\frac{9}{16}$ in.) long.

92a. Leaves glaucous; Cascade Mts., s WA, to Deschutes Co., OR. **79. P. euglaucus p. 180**

92b. Leaves green; e of Cascades, cent WA to w-cent MT, n WY, n NM, the Sierras of CA and the n end of the Willamette Valley and adjacent sw WA. **80. P. rydbergii p. 182**

A1. Calyx 5 to 8 mm long; corolla 13 to 20 mm ($\frac{1}{2}$–$\frac{13}{16}$ in.) long; foliage finely pubescent; se ID, sw WY, UT and n AZ. **P. rydbergii var. aggregatus**

A2. Calyx 3 to 6 mm long, corolla 10 to 14 mm ($\frac{3}{8}$–$\frac{9}{16}$ in.) long, foliage glabrous or finely pubescent.

B1. Sepals broadly scarious and deeply erose-toothed; foliage finely pubescent; se WA and ne OR, cent ID and sw MT. **P. rydbergii var. rydbergii**

B2. Sepals slightly scarious and entire or shallowly erose; foliage glabrous; Cascade-Sierras of OR and CA to nw NV. **P. rydbergii var. oreocharis**

1. *PENSTEMON BARRETTIAE* GRAY
Barrett's Penstemon

The feminine Latin ending -*iae* in this case indicates a woman's connection to this penstemon. Indeed, *P. barrettiae* memorializes Almeta Hodge Barrett, a doctor's wife, who lived in Hood River, Oregon, in the late nineteenth century. Little is known of Mrs. Barrett, except that she discovered her flower prior to 1886 when Asa Gray first described *Penstemon barrettiae*.

This plant forms dense clumps. The leafy foliage has a pretty bluish-green-glaucous coating. Numerous sterile or nonflowering leafy stems usually grow at the base. A wildflower planting area on Interstate 84 off the westbound lane between The Dalles and Hood River, Oregon, features a beautiful stand of *Penstemon barrettiae*.

Stems: Length 1.5 to 4 dm (6–16 in.), generally spreading to prostrate and often mat-forming.

Leaves: 4 to 8 cm (1½–3 in.) long, including short petioles at the base of the plant, lanceolate to elliptic and 2.5 cm (1 in.) broad, entire to irregularly serrate on the margins; cauline (stem) leaves smaller and sessile to clasping, all glabrous and glaucous.

Inflorescence: A raceme or a panicle usually with 2 flowers per cyme.

Calyx: 5 to 8 mm (to 5/16 in.) long, the sepals ovate, tapered to acute tips and entire to erose on the margins.

Corolla: 2.5 to 3.8 cm (1–1½ in.) long and 1 cm (3/8 in.) wide at the mouth, keeled on top and 2-ridged on the palate within, lilac or rose-purple, the lips relatively short and the palate copiously white-bearded.

Anther Sacs: Densely white-woolly, explanate, and diverging or becoming opposite.

Staminode: Naked and included within the corolla, about 1/2 the length of the fertile stamens.

Blooming: April and May.

Habitat/Range: Basalt cliffs and talus slopes at lower elevations in the east end of the Columbia Gorge.

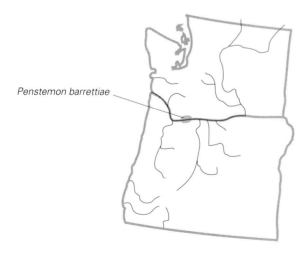

Penstemon barrettiae

Penstemon barrettiae

Penstemon barrettiae

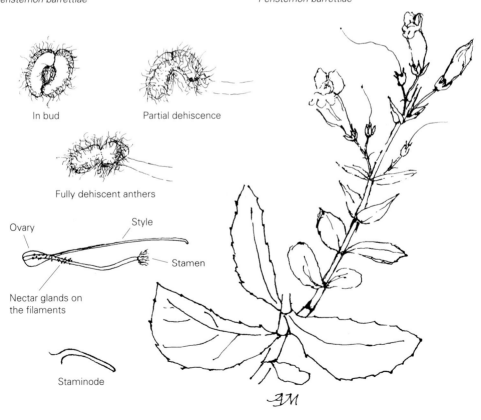

In bud

Partial dehiscence

Fully dehiscent anthers

Ovary

Style

Stamen

Nectar glands on
the filaments

Staminode

2. *PENSTEMON RUPICOLA* (PIPER) HOWELL
Rock Penstemon

This vibrant red penstemon roots in cracks in rock cliffs or outcrops. One can see it by climbing the steps up Beacon Rock in the Columbia Gorge or by taking a short walk to the summit of Larch Mountain on the Oregon side of the gorge. Wherever you find them, please do not pick the flowers. Leave them for others and future generations to enjoy.

Stems: Shrubby at the base, prostrate and matted against the rocky substrate; stems rising 1 dm (4 in.) tall or less, very leafy and short-hairy.

Leaves: Ovate, leathery, bluish-glaucous, minutely to markedly serrate, 8 to 18 mm ($^1/_4$–$^{11}/_{16}$ in.) long; cauline leaves much reduced.

Inflorescence: A raceme, few-flowered and compact, secund (on one side of the stem) and glandular-pubescent.

Calyx: Sepals elliptic, 6 to 11 mm ($^1/_4$–$^1/_2$ in.) long, glandular, acute at the tip and often purplish.

Corolla: Pink to deep rose, 2.5 to 3.7 cm (1–1$^1/_2$ in.) long and rather narrow, keeled on top, 2-ridged on the palate within, glabrous except for perhaps a few hairs on the palate and broadly 2-lipped.

Anther Sacs: Densely woolly-pubescent, explanate, mostly included within the corolla or slightly exserted.

Staminode: Glabrous or sparsely bearded, short and included.

Blooming: Late spring to midsummer, depending on elevation.

Habitat: Basalt rock cliffs or rock outcrops from low elevation in the Columbia Gorge to high in the mountains.

Range: The Cascades on both east and west slopes from s Washington to sw Oregon and n California.

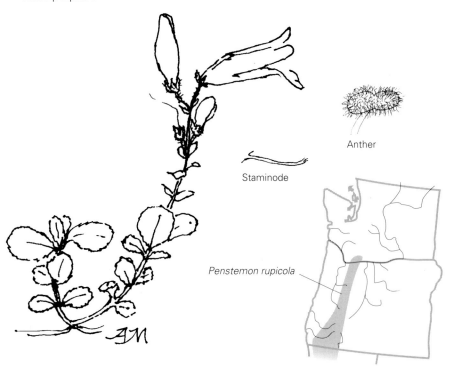

Anther

Staminode

Penstemon rupicola

Penstemon rupicola

3. *PENSTEMON NEWBERRYI* VAR. *BERRYI* (EASTW.) KECK
Mountain Pride, Berry's Penstemon

This penstemon is named for John S. Newberry, a nineteenth-century plant collector, and the variety for Samuel S. Berry. It is basically a n California species that ranges into sw Oregon. The flowers of variety *berryi* that I observed were lavender to pale purple, but other authors describe them as being pink. The color photographs taken by the author came out pinkish, because color film often reacts more strongly to the red component of the flower than to the blue component. As noted by Lodewick (1994), *Penstemon newberryi* var. *berryi* is probably more closely related to *P. cardwellii* than to *P. newberryi* and should perhaps be named *Penstemon cardwellii* var. *berryi* instead. This name change is only a suggestion, however. The type variety, *Penstemon newberryi* var. *newberryi,* on the other hand, occurs only in northern California and northwestern Nevada. The picture shown of it was taken on Mt. Shasta in northern California and is NOT var. *berryi.* It has exserted stamens appearing as white spots in the throats of the corollas. The red or pink color shown in the small photo is typical of this variety.

Stems: Branching at the base, reclining and somewhat mat-forming, 1.2 to 3 dm (5–12 in.) long, often with leafy, sterile side branches.

Leaves: Larger leaves grow on the base of the stems and on sterile shoots, to 4 cm (1 1/2 in.) long, ovate, elliptic or oar-shaped on short petioles, glabrous or feebly pubescent, serrate to nearly entire on the margins; upper cauline leaves greatly reduced to mere bracts.

Inflorescence: A few-flowered raceme, glandular and more or less secund.

Calyx: 7 to 12 mm (to 1/2 in.) long, the sepals lanceolate to ovate, green, glandular and tapered to acute tips.

Corolla: 2.5 to 3+ cm (1–1 1/4 in.) long, gaping at the mouth, lavender to purplish or pinkish, glabrous outside, keeled on the top and 2-ridged on the bottom within, modestly white-bearded on the palate.

Anther Sacs: Densely long woolly and white, the lobes spreading opposite and explanate, just reaching the mouth of the corolla.

Staminode: Slender, modestly bearded with pale yellow pubescence, short and included.

Blooming: June to August.

Habitat: Rocky outcrops and talus slopes, moderate to high elevations in the mountains.

Range: Josephine Co., Oregon, and n California.

Penstemon newberryi var. *berryi*

Penstemon newberryi var. *berryi*

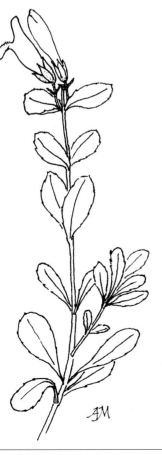

Penstemon newberryi var. *newberryi*
(photographed in n CA)

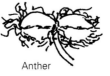

Anther

Staminode

4. *PENSTEMON LYALLII* GRAY
Lyall's Penstemon

Penstemon lyallii is named for David Lyall, an early botanist and plant collector in the Northwest. The species is very distinctive with its relatively long, narrow and pointed leaves and open, branching inflorescence. It is known to hybridize with *P. ellipticus* near the Montana–British Columbia border, where both parent species occur together. However, the hybrids do not seem to be self-fertile, because in other places where both species occur at short distances from each other there are no hybrids. *Penstemon lyallii* may also hybridize with *P. fruticosus,* but the ranges of the two do not overlap much if at all.

Stems: Shrubby only at the base, the plants entirely herbaceous above, 3 to 8 dm (12–32 in.) tall, glabrous below the inflorescence.

Leaves: Deciduous, all cauline, 3 to 13 cm (1–5 in.) long and narrow, approximately 10 times as long as wide, sharp-pointed, pale green and nearly entire to finely serrate.

Inflorescence: An open, spreading panicle, glandular-pubescent.

Calyx: Sepals narrow, 7 to 15 mm (to $^5/_8$ in.) long, glandular, entire and acute.

Corolla: Pale lavender, 3 to 4 cm ($1^1/_4$–$1^1/_2$ in.) long, bearded on the two ridges of the palate and glabrous outside.

Anther Sacs: Woolly pubescent, explanate.

Staminode: Short, glabrous, not much expanded at the tip.

Blooming: June to August.

Habitat: Steep, rocky mountainsides and rock outcrops to gravel bars at streamside, subalpine and alpine.

Range: Southeastern British Columbia, sw Alberta, n Idaho and nw Montana.

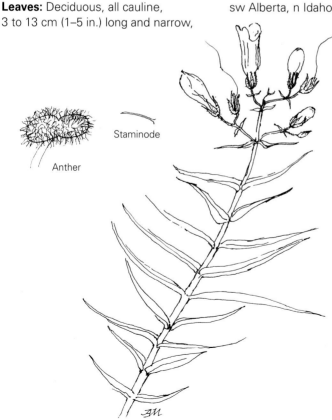

Staminode

Anther

Penstemon lyallii

Penstemon lyallii

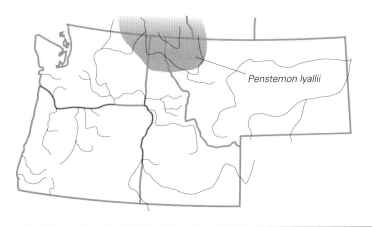

Penstemon lyallii

5. *NOTHOCHELONE NEMOROSA* (DOUGL. EX LINDL.) STRAW
(Penstemon nemorosus [Dougl. ex Lindl.] Traut.)
Woodland Beardtongue, Turtlehead

This near-relative of penstemons has now been placed alone in its own genus. It differs from *Penstemon* in bearing nectary glands on a disk below the ovary, instead of on minute glandular hairs beside the ovary. The name *nemorosa* means "in the woods."

Stems: Glabrous or very finely pubescent, herbaceous, usually several stems arising from a woody root crown, 4 to 8 dm (16–32 in.) long, upright or reclining.

Leaves: All attached to the flowering stems, the lower ones smaller than those above, thin, green, toothed on the margins, lanceolate to ovate, to 11 cm (4^1/$_2$ in.) long.

Inflorescence: A glandular panicle, usually secund.

Calyx: 6 to 10 mm (^{1}/$_4$–^{3}/$_8$ in.) long, the sepals entire and lance-shaped.

Corolla: 2.5 to 3.3 cm (1–1^5/$_{16}$ in.) long, somewhat flattened, glandular outside, glabrous within, bright pinkish purple.

Anther Sacs: Densely woolly, becoming dehiscent full length and explanate, the filaments finely pubescent at the base.

Staminode: Bearded full length and short.

Blooming: In the summer.

Habitat: Forest openings and scattered woods where rocky, from low to moderately high elevations in the mountains.

Range: Vancouver Island and w Washington to nw California, the Cascades to the coast.

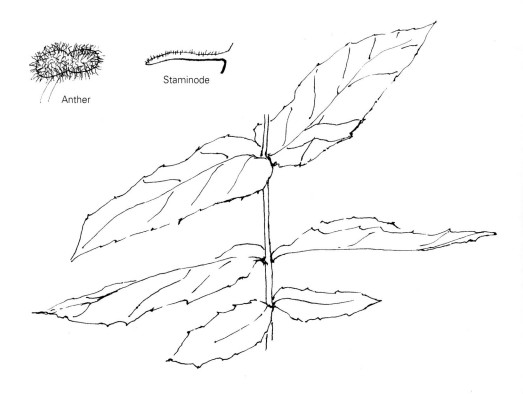

Anther

Staminode

Nothochelone nemorosa

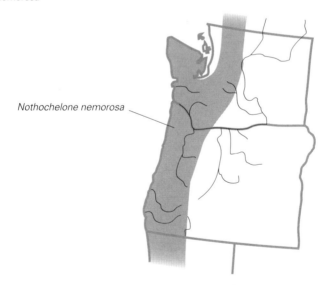

Nothochelone nemorosa

6. *PENSTEMON MONTANUS* GREENE
Mountain Penstemon, Cordroot Penstemon

This lovely penstemon has two easily distinguished varieties. Var. *montanus* displays toothed leaves that are mostly glandular-pubescent, while var. *idahoensis* possesses mostly entire, nonglandular leaves. *Penstemon montanus* is an alpine inhabitant that may require considerable work to find, but the mountain climber is richly rewarded by the effort.

Stems: Woody at the base and branching, somewhat mat-forming, often resembling aerial runners, spreading and more or less prostrate; flowering, cauline stems herbaceous, 1 to 3 dm (4–12 in.) long and upright, some leafy, sterile stems usually equal to the fertile ones.

Leaves: To 5 cm (2 in.) long, smaller below and all cauline, varying from glabrous to glandular and sharply serrate to entire and green or glaucous, depending on the variety.

Inflorescence: Normally 2 flowers per node except 1 terminal; a crowded, secund raceme without subtending bracts, glandular or glabrous.

Calyx: 8 to 14 mm ($^5/_{16}$–$^9/_{16}$ in.) long, the sepals narrow, acute, entire on the margins and mostly glandular.

Corolla: 2.6 to 3.9 cm (1–1$^1/_2$ in.) long, blue, lavender or violet, glabrous, keeled on top and bearded on the 2-ridged palate.

Anther Sacs: Densely white-woolly, the sacs becoming opposite and explanate.

Staminode: Slender, short and included within the corolla, glabrous or lightly bearded $^1/_2$ length.

Blooming: Mostly in midsummer.

Habitat: Subalpine and alpine on rocky outcrops or talus.

Range: Central Idaho to s-central Montana, w Wyoming and central Utah.

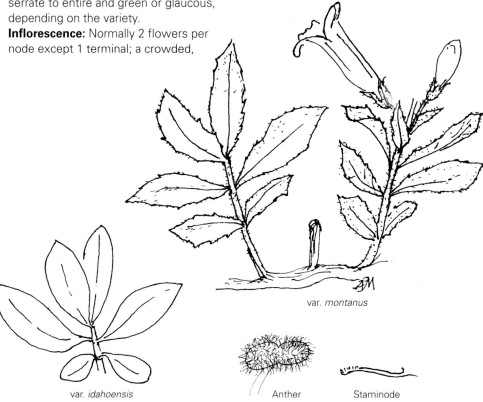

var. *montanus*

var. *idahoensis*

Anther

Staminode

Penstemon montanus var. *montanus*

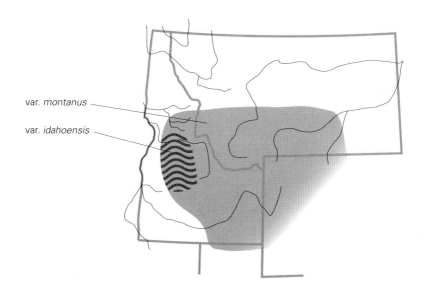

var. *montanus*

var. *idahoensis*

7. *PENSTEMON ELLIPTICUS* COULT. AND FISH.
Rockvine Penstemon

Ellipticus means "bearing elliptic leaves." This species could be considered a variety of *Penstemon davidsonii,* but the robust leaves on the flowering stems of *ellipticus* distinctly differentiate the two species. *Penstemon ellipticus* sometimes hybridizes with *P. lyallii* and perhaps with *fruticosus.* In the latter case the ranges of the two species do not overlap to an appreciable extent. The hybrids, where they do occur, do not seem to spread far from the parent species.

Stems: The basal stems woody, prostrate and often rooting by layering and forming substantial mats; the flowering stems reach 5 to 15 cm (2–6 in.) long and are quite pubescent.

Leaves: Elliptic to ovate, 1 to 2.5 cm (to 1 in.) long and usually on short petioles, glabrous and round or obtuse on the end, usually finely serrate on the margins, some leaves evergreen and others deciduous.

Inflorescence: A glandular raceme.

Calyx: The sepals narrow, lanceolate to oblong, 8 to 15 mm ($^5/_{16}$–$^5/_8$ in.) long.

Corolla: Deep lavender, 2.7 to 4 cm (1–1$^1/_2$ in.) long, glabrous without and white-hairy on the palate within, keeled on top and 2-ridged on the palate.

Anther Sacs: Woolly-pubescent and explanate.

Staminode: Slender, short, included within the corolla and well-bearded.

Blooming: In the summer.

Habitat: Rocky places, mostly alpine.

Range: Southeastern British Columbia and sw Alberta, n Idaho and nw Montana, rare in central Idaho and sw Montana.

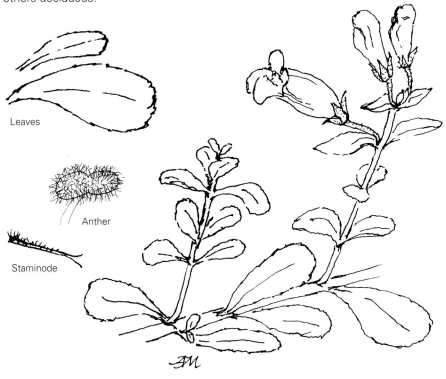

Leaves

Anther

Staminode

Penstemon ellipticus

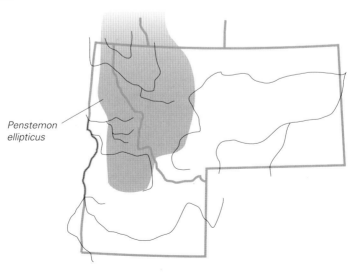

Penstemon
ellipticus

8. *PENSTEMON DAVIDSONII* GREENE
(*Penstemon menziesii* Hook.)
Davidson's Penstemon, Creeping Penstemon

This species is named for George Davidson, an early plant collector. It exhibits three or, according to some authors, four varieties. The fourth variety is treated here as a more robust form of var. *menziesii* in the east-central Washington Cascades. Variety *davidsonii* has entire leaves and generally is found from Mt. Rainier to the California Sierras. Variety *menziesii* has somewhat serrate leaves and occurs from sw British Columbia to the northern Oregon Cascades. A larger-flowered variety, *praeteritus,* with short points at leaf tips, can be found on Steens Mountain of se Oregon.

Stems: Shrubby at the base and mat-forming, the flowering stems from less than 10 to 15 cm (to 6 in.) high.

Leaves: Mostly basal, to 1.5 cm (to ⅝ in.) long, elliptical to nearly round, green, glabrous and quite thick; cauline leaves few and much smaller to bractlike.

Inflorescence: A compact, few-flowered raceme, secund and usually glandular.

Calyx: The sepals narrow to ovate, 7 to 15 mm (to ⅝ in.) long, obtuse to acute and green.

Corolla: Blue to lavender or purple, 2.5 to 4 cm (1–1½+ in.) long, keeled on top and 2-ridged on the palate, glabrous outside and the palate sparsely to densely bearded.

Anther Sacs: White-woolly and fully dehiscent.

Staminode: Short, about ½ as long as the stamen filaments and bearded at the tip.

Blooming: In the summer.

Habitat: Rocky outcrops or talus from montane to alpine.

Range: Coastal British Columbia through Coast and Cascade ranges to the California Sierras and on Steens Mountain, Oregon.

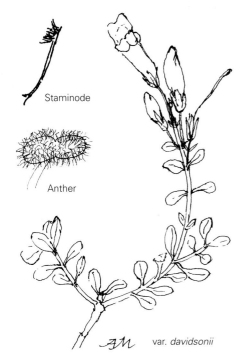

Staminode

Anther

var. *davidsonii*

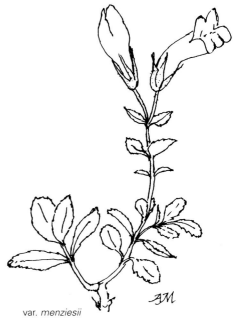

var. *menziesii*

P. davidsonii var. *praeteritus*

P. davidsonii var. *davidsonii*

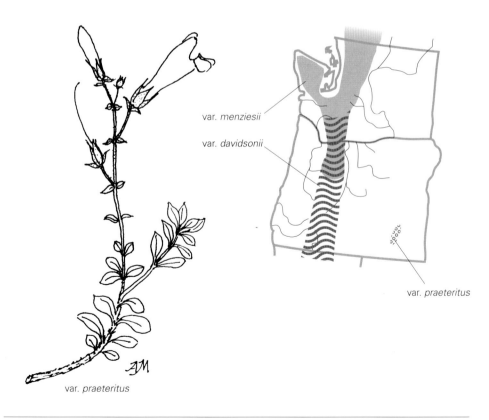

var. *menziesii*

var. *davidsonii*

var. *praeteritus*

var. *praeteritus*

9. *PENSTEMON FRUTICOSUS* (PURSH) GREENE
Shrubby Penstemon, Bush Penstemon

Fruticosus means "shrubby" or "woody" and this species is perhaps the woodiest of all the penstemons. Three varieties, differing mainly in the leaves, are generally recognized as follows: var. *serratus* has small, markedly toothed leaves and occurs in the Blue Mountains and adjacent west-central Idaho; var. *scouleri* has linear or narrow leaves that are mostly entire in n Idaho, ne Washington and adjacent British Columbia; and var. *fruticosus*, with broader leaves, occupies the rest of the range.

Stems: Woody and freely branched, generally prostrate and mat-forming at the base, with numerous sterile branches usually present; the flowering stems erect and 1.5 to 4 dm (6–16 in.) high, the plants sometimes forming extensive colonies.

Leaves: Vary according to the variety as described above, evergreen, rather leathery and shiny green, the cauline leaves much smaller than those at the base.

Inflorescence: A few-flowered, secund, glandular raceme.

Calyx: Glandular, the sepals entire, herbaceous, variable shape, but generally acute at the tip, 7 to 15 mm (to ⅝ in.) long.

Corolla: Blue-lavender to purplish, 2.5 to 5 cm (1–2 in.) long, glabrous outside and bearded white or yellowish on the 2-ridged palate, the lower lip longer than the upper.

Anther Sacs: Densely woolly, white, totally dehiscent and explanate.

Staminode: About ½ the length of the filaments, yellow-bearded at the slender tip.

Blooming: May to August.

Habitat: Open rocky slopes to moderately dense forest, from the foothills to the high mountains.

Range: From the Cascade Summit in s British Columbia to sw Alberta, w Montana and Wyoming to central Oregon.

Staminode

Anther

var. *serratus*

var. *scouleri*

P. fruticosus
var. scouleri

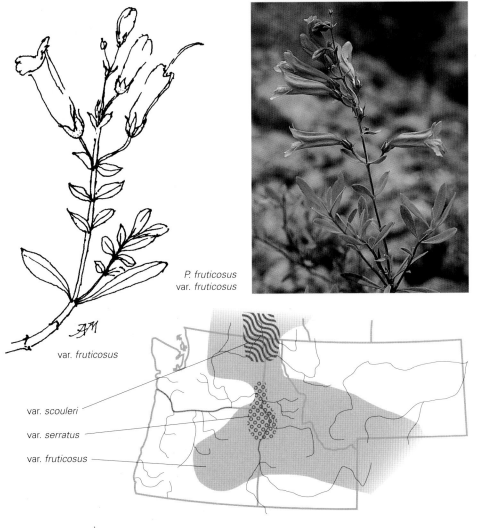

P. fruticosus
var. fruticosus

var. fruticosus

var. scouleri

var. serratus

var. fruticosus

10. *PENSTEMON CARDWELLII* HOWELL
Cardwell's Penstemon

This species is named for Dr. James R. Cardwell (1830–1916), horticulturist, musician and the first dentist to practice in Portland, Oregon. He emigrated to Oregon by wagon in 1851 and actively participated in plant science activities in the fledgling state. *Penstemon cardwellii* is closely related to *P. fruticosus* and was considered to be a variety of that taxon at one time. It occurs abundantly near the end of the road to the viewpoint below Mt. St. Helens, on Washington Highway 504.

Stems: Shrubby at the base, 1 to 3 dm (4–12 in.) long, lax and somewhat mat-forming, sometimes rooting by layering; flowering stems 1 to 2 dm (4–8 in.) long, glabrous below the inflorescence.

Leaves: Basal leaves 1.5 to 4 cm (⁵/₈–1¹/₂ in.) long including a short petiole, elliptic and rounded or obtuse at the end, entire or remotely serrate on the margins, glabrous; cauline leaves much smaller but broad and sessile.

Inflorescence: Normally a crowded, few-flowered raceme, sparsely glandular.

Calyx: 7 to 12 mm (³/₈–¹/₂ in.) long, the sepals lanceolate to ovate and tapering to acute tips.

Corolla: Blue-violet to purple, 2.5 to 3.8 cm (1–1¹/₂ in.) long and about 1 cm wide at the mouth, the tube proper (the base of the corolla before it expands) shorter than the calyx, keeled, 2-ridged and long-hairy on the palate, glabrous outside.

Anther Sacs: Woolly-hairy, becoming opposite and explanate.

Staminode: Very slender, short, included and sparsely yellow-bearded with rather long hairs.

Blooming: May to July or early August.

Habitat: Openings or wooded slopes at moderate elevations in the mountains.

Range: Cascade Mountains of sw Washington and Oregon, to the Coast Range in Oregon.

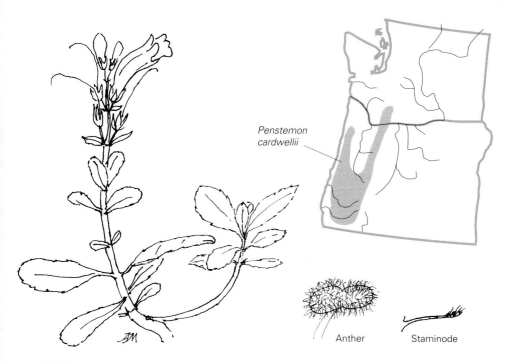

Penstemon cardwellii

Anther   Staminode

Penstemon cardwellii

11. *PENSTEMON GLANDULOSUS* DOUGL. EX LINDL.
Glandular Penstemon, Sticky-stem Penstemon

The unmistakable feature of this penstemon is the sticky, gland-tipped pubescence on most parts of the plant. The stems and inflorescence are especially glandular, while the lower leaf blades may be nearly glabrous. Two well-separated varieties compose this outstanding species. It has not been recognized as an especially good "garden variety" to date, but it may offer excellent prospects for cultivation, especially the variety *chelanensis*.

Stems: Several stout, upright stems reach 4 to 10 dm (16–40 in.) high, densely glandular full length.

Leaves: Basal leaves generally 1 to 3.5 dm (4–14 in.) long, the petiole making about ⅓ the length, 2.5 to 9 cm (1–3½ in.) wide, more or less glandular, dentate in var. *glandulosus* and entire in var. *chelanensis*, usually lanceolate; cauline leaves smaller, sessile to clasping, lanceolate to broadly ovate.

Inflorescence: Densely glandular, of 2 to 6 well-separated verticillasters, composed of several to many flowers.

Calyx: The sepals narrowly lanceolate, glandular, 9 to 15 mm long, acute at the tip and herbaceous with entire margins.

Corolla: Glandular outside but glabrous inside, 2.5 to 4.5 cm (1–1¾ in.) long, blue-lavender to violet with darker guide lines and a white beard on the palate, expanded to 1.1 to 1.5 cm (about ½ in.) wide at the throat.

Anther Sacs: Broader than long, dehiscent across the connective, remaining saccate at the ends and parallel, with distinct teeth on the sutures, the pollen sacs 1.7 to 2.3 mm long.

Staminode: Glabrous, expanded and flattened at the tip, reaching the orifice or slightly exserted.

Blooming: May to July.

Habitat: Open, rocky hillsides and canyons to scattered timber in the mountains.

Range: Southeastern Washington and ne Oregon to sw Idaho (var. *glandulosus*), disjunct along the east slope of the Cascades from Chelan Co., Washington, to Hood River Co., Oregon (var. *chelanensis*).

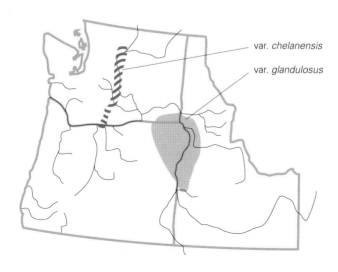

var. *chelanensis*

var. *glandulosus*

P. glandulosus var. *glandulosus*

P. glandulosus var. *chelanensis*

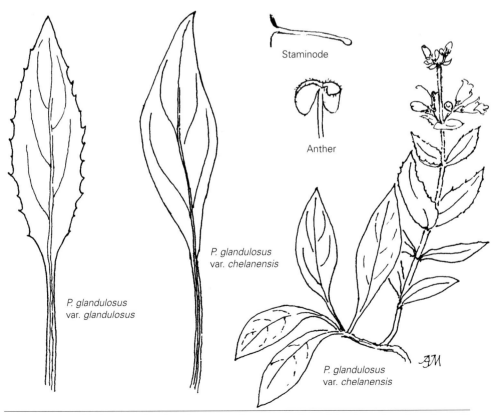

Staminode

Anther

P. glandulosus
var. *chelanensis*

P. glandulosus
var. *glandulosus*

P. glandulosus
var. *chelanensis*

(Anther sacs closed on the outer ends, permanently parallel or horseshoe-shaped) • **45**

12. *PENSTEMON TRIPHYLLUS* DOUGL.
Whorled Penstemon

The name *triphyllus* alludes to the obvious feature of this penstemon—the 3- or 4-whorled leaves at well-spaced nodes along the middle stems. Upper stems usually have some opposite or scattered leaves as well. Also the leaves are gray-green from a combination of a glaucous coating and fine pubescence. *Penstemon triphyllus* could also be called Snake River or Hell's Canyon penstemon because of its primary range.

Stems: Numerous, slender and brittle, growing in a bushy clump.

Leaves: All cauline (without a basal rosette), mostly 3- or 4-whorled but a few opposite or scattered, glabrous or minutely pubescent and glaucous, linear to lanceolate, irregularly toothed or cleft, 2.5 to 5 cm (1–2 in.) long, the lower leaves reduced.

Inflorescence: An open, scattered, mixed raceme-panicle, glandular.

Calyx: Green or purplish, the sepals 4 to 6 mm (to ¼ in.) long, often quite unequal in size, entire on the margins, lanceolate to ovate and glandular.

Corolla: Blue-lavender to lilac with prominent guide lines, glandular outside but glabrous inside, a gradually spreading tube 1.5 to 2 cm (½–¾ in.) long, usually with a light beard on the palate.

Stamens: Anthers about 1 mm long and as broad as long, the sacs permanently horseshoe-shaped, dehiscing about ⅓ their length at the inner ends across the connective, glabrous on the valves and finely toothed along the sutures.

Staminode: Well-bearded with yellow hairs and exserted out of the corolla throat.

Blooming: May to July.

Habitat: Basalt cliffs and rocky talus slopes at lower elevations.

Range: Hell's Canyon and the lower Snake River Canyon in Washington, the lower tributaries to this reach of the Snake River and a short stretch of the Columbia River below the Snake confluence.

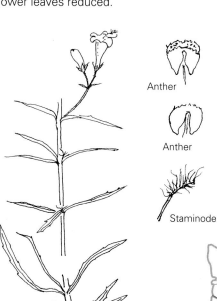

Anther

Anther

Staminode

Penstemon triphyllus

Penstemon triphyllus

(Anther sacs closed on the outer ends, permanently parallel or horseshoe-shaped) • **47**

13. *PENSTEMON RICHARDSONII* DOUGL. EX LINDL.
Cut-leaved Penstemon, Richardson's Penstemon

Named in the early nineteenth century for a John Richardson, this species includes three varieties that are rather poorly differentiated because they frequently intergrade into each other. Variety *curtiflorus* has corollas no more than 2 cm (¹³/₁₆ in.) long and glabrous staminodes, whereas the other two have longer blossoms and lightly bearded sterile stamens. Variety *richardsonii* has narrow, deeply toothed or cleft leaves, while the leaves of var. *dentatus* are broader, lanceolate and more shallowly and regularly dentate.

Stems: Few to numerous in a bushy clump, 2 to 8 dm (8–32 in.) high, rather slender and brittle, often lax and sprawling, quite shrubby at the base.

Leaves: Vary with the variety from deeply cleft to regularly toothed or dentate, the blades 2.5 to 5 cm (1–2 in.) long, all cauline, mostly glabrous to lightly nonglandular-pubescent.

Inflorescence: A raceme or a mixed raceme-panicle, generally uncrowded, glandular and somewhat leafy.

Calyx: 4 to 9 mm long, the sepals lance-shaped to ovate and often unequal in size, green or purplish, the margins mostly entire.

Corolla: Glandular outside to glabrous or with a few hairs inside, pink to lavender or blue with prominent darker guide lines on the palate, the tube expanded to a broad throat, not strongly 2-lipped.

Anther Sacs: Dehisce only ¹/₃ to ¹/₂ their length, across the confluent ends and the connective, remaining horseshoe-shaped, minutely toothed on the sutures.

Staminode: Bearded or glabrous and slightly exserted.

Blooming: May to August.

Habitat: Open rocky places, rock slides to cliff faces.

Range: Southern British Columbia to central Oregon, e of the Cascade Crest and along the Columbia and Snake rivers to e Washington.

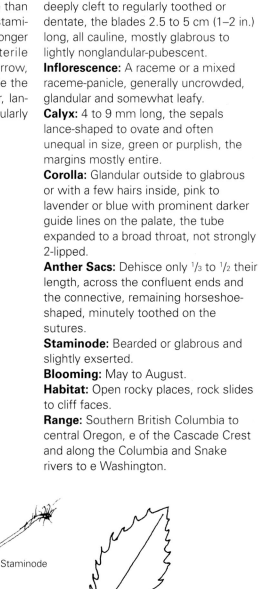

Staminode

var. *dentatus*

P. richardsonii var. *dentatus*

P. richardsonii var. *richardsonii*

var. *richardsonii*

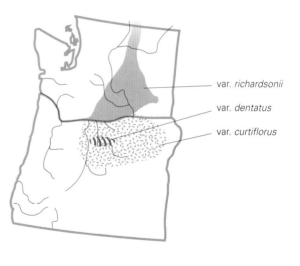

var. *richardsonii*
var. *dentatus*
var. *curtiflorus*

14. *PENSTEMON DIPHYLLUS* RYDB.
Two-leaved Penstemon

Diphyllus means "two-leaved" and the species is closely related to *P. triphyllus*. At one time it was considered to be a subspecies of *triphyllus*. This rather uncommon species is also rather closely allied to *P. richardsonii,* as evidenced by the toothed leaves as well as other similar features.

Stems: Usually a few in a clump, woody at the base, finely pubescent below the inflorescence, 1.5 to 6 dm (6–24 in.) long, more or less upright or sprawling.

Leaves: Rather irregularly toothed, 2 to 8 cm (1-3 in.) long, all cauline, mostly sessile, the lower leaves smaller than the upper, glabrous.

Inflorescence: Glandular, a branching, leafy-bracted, uncrowded, mixed raceme-panicle.

Calyx: Glandular, green or purple, 4 to 6 mm (to ¼ in.) long, the sepals narrow and often unequal in size, entire on the margins.

Corolla: Lavender to violet, glandular outside and glabrous within except for a few hairs on the palate, 1.3 to 1.9 cm (½ to ¾ in.) long, not much expanded at the throat, the upper lip notched about ½ its length.

Anthers: Permanently horseshoe-shaped, 0.9 to 1.3 mm long, dehiscent across the connective and pouched at the outer ends, with minute teeth along the sutures.

Staminode: Bearded ⅓ to ½ its length, somewhat expanded at the tip and slightly exserted from the corolla.

Blooming: Late June to July.

Habitat: Rocky slopes and cliffs at lower elevations in the mountains.

Range: Western Montana, n and central Idaho and apparently disjunct at Palouse Falls in sw Washington.

Staminode

Anther

Penstemon diphyllus

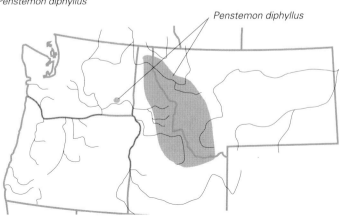

Penstemon diphyllus

15. *PENSTEMON SERRULATUS* MENZIES EX SMITH
(*Penstemon diffusus* Lindl.)
Cascade Penstemon, Coast Penstemon

Penstemon serrulatus occurs in wetter habitats than most species, but still requires moderately good soil drainage in places that dry out by late summer. The name *serrulatus* refers to the finely serrate leaf margins.

Stems: Several rise in a clump from a woody base, 2 to 7 dm (8–28 in.) high, glabrous at the base, but often minutely pubescent above.

Leaves: All attached to the stem (cauline), 2 to 9 cm ($^3/_4$–$3^1/_2$ in.) long on short petioles below, smaller and sessile or clasping above, almost entire to markedly serrate, the blades broadly lanceolate or elliptic to heart-shaped.

Inflorescence: Most commonly a single, densely crowded thyrse at the apex to as many as 5 well-spaced verticillasters, the lower clusters, if present, on peduncles closely pressed against the stem, finely nonglandular-hairy.

Calyx: 5 to 11 mm (to $^3/_8$ in.) long, the sepals narrow to ovate, the margins very finely pubescent (ciliolate).

Corolla: A short tube at the base that expands abruptly to a longer, broad limb, strongly 2-lipped, 1.6 to 2.5 cm ($^5/_8$–1 in.) long, deep blue to purple, glabrous throughout or with a sparse beard on the palate.

Anthers: Glabrous, dehiscent about $^1/_2$ length, the sutures very finely toothed.

Staminode: Yellow-bearded about $^1/_2$ length, expanded and flattened at the tip and exserted slightly out of the corolla.

Blooming: June to early August.

Habitat: Moist ground in the spring in forest openings to wooded slopes from sea level to 6,000 ft. elevation.

Range: Southern Alaska and sw British Columbia to nw Oregon, w of the Cascade Crest.

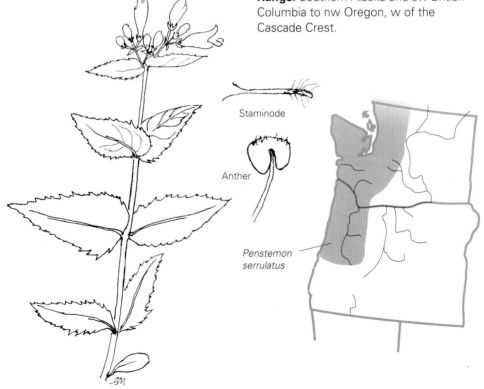

Staminode

Anther

Penstemon serrulatus

Penstemon serrulatus

16. *PENSTEMON VENUSTUS* DOUGL.
Lovely Penstemon, Beautiful Penstemon

Lovely penstemon is unique with its long, flexuous pubescence on the filaments just below the anthers. This characteristic immediately identifies *Penstemon venustus*. The name *venustus* means "beautiful" or "graceful." It occurs quite commonly in the dry canyons and other rocky sites within its range.

Stems: Few to many, growing in large clumps, 3 to 8 dm (12–32 in.) tall, glabrous except for occasional lines of fine pubescence along the main axes originating in leaf axils.

Leaves: All cauline, 4 to 10 cm (1¹/₂–4 in.) long, sessile, rarely entire, mostly dentate or finely serrate with very short, soft spines at the ends of the teeth, glabrous, the lower leaves reduced, lanceolate to oblong and acute at the tip.

Inflorescence: A glabrous mixed raceme-panicle, usually quite secund.

Calyx: White-margined (scarious) and erose or raggedly toothed, 3 to 6 mm (to ¹/₄ in.) long.

Corolla: Mostly lavender to violet or purplish, glabrous both inside and out, 2 to 3.8 cm (³/₄–1¹/₂ in.) long, distinctly 2-lipped, the petal lobe margins lined with very fine hairs.

Stamens: The filaments markedly pubescent with long white hairs near the top, the anthers horseshoe-shaped, the sacs 1.6 to 2 mm long and dehiscent across the contiguous ends about ¹/₂ to ¹/₃ their length, somewhat exserted from the corolla throat.

Staminode: White-bearded at the expanded and flattened tip and shortly exserted.

Blooming: May into August.

Habitat: Open rock outcrops and gravelly or talus slopes from valleys to subalpine in the mountains.

Range: The Blue Mountains of se Washington and ne Oregon and adjacent w-central Idaho. Reportedly naturalized from cultivation in California.

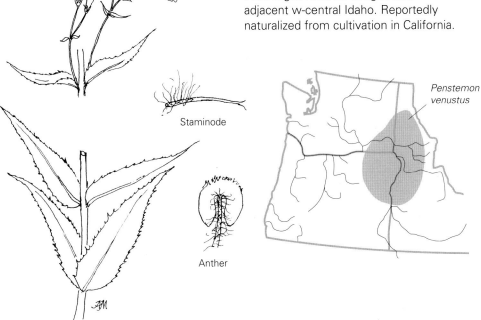

Staminode

Anther

Penstemon venustus

Penstemon venustus

Penstemon venustus

17. *PENSTEMON GRACILENTUS* A. GRAY
Very Slender Penstemon

Gracilentus means "slender and flexible," referring to the stems. The species is quite rare in Oregon, but more common in ne California and Nevada.

Stems: Upright, usually several in a clump from a woody root crown, sometimes with nonflowering (sterile) shoots at the base, 2 to 7 dm (8–28 in.) tall, glabrous and somewhat glaucous in the inflorescence.

Leaves: Mostly cauline, but crowded near the base, widely spaced and much reduced above, lanceolate to spatulate below, linear to narrow lanceolate above, glabrous, green or sometimes glaucous and entire on the margins.

Inflorescence: Glandular especially on the pedicels and calyces, a well-spaced panicle of 3 to 5 verticillasters, the cymes 2- to 4-flowered, the lower cymes long-peduncled and moderately spreading from the stems.

Calyx: The sepals lanceolate and glandular, 3 to 6 mm ($^1/_4$ in.) long.

Corolla: Reddish purple to bluish purple, keeled on top and 2-ridged on the palate, glandular outside and glabrous inside to rather densely pubescent on the palate, not strongly 2-lipped, the lower lip straight in line with the tube, the upper lip divergent.

Anthers: Brown to dark purple, dehiscing about $^1/_2$ length across the connected ends, the sutures lightly toothed, the sacs remaining parallel and horseshoe-shaped and pouched on the ends.

Staminode: Yellow-bearded at the tip and included within the corolla.

Blooming: June to August.

Habitat: Sagebrush slopes and flats on lava and granitic soils into the mountains.

Range: Mountains of s Lake Co., Oregon, ne California and nw Nevada, south to Lake Tahoe.

Staminode

Anther

Penstemon gracilentus

Penstemon gracilentus

18. *PENSTEMON KINGII* S. WATSON
King's Penstemon

Penstemon kingii is named for George King, a latter nineteenth-century western explorer. It is an uncommon, if not rare, species, native mostly to the mountains of northern Nevada. This pretty little penstemon is distinguished by the velvety, ashy green color of the herbage that results from nonglandular hairs. Only the outer corolla, calyx and the adjacent upper pedicels bear glandular hairs.

Stems: Ashy-colored from a coating of short, spreading pubescence; 7 to 25 cm (3–10 in.) long, several stems spreading from the base and turning upright at the ends.

Leaves: All cauline, ashy gray-green, entire, mostly linear to oblanceolate, commonly channeled and arched, 2 to 4 cm (³/₄–1¹/₂ in.) long, with narrow bases approximating short petioles on the lower stems.

Inflorescence: A panicle of 4 to 10 crowded verticillasters, often appearing as a continuous thyrse, the cymes 2- to 4-flowered.

Calyx: The sepals narrow-lanceolate and acute, 4 to 8 mm (to ⁵/₁₆ in.) long, glandular, purple or green, the margins entire and narrowly scarious.

Corolla: Inflated (bellied) on the lower side, 1.4 to 2.2 cm (⁵/₈–⁷/₈ in.) long, dark violet to reddish violet or purple and often shading to white at the base, glandular outside and glabrous including the palate within, the top of the pedicel glandular.

Anther Sacs: Dehiscing narrowly across the confluent ends, permanently horseshoe-shaped, the sutures finely toothed, purple to black and slightly exserted.

Staminode: Glabrous, somewhat expanded at the tip and slightly exserted.

Blooming: Mostly in June.

Habitat: Sagebrush flats and hills into the mountains.

Range: Southern Malheur Co., Oregon, and n Nevada.

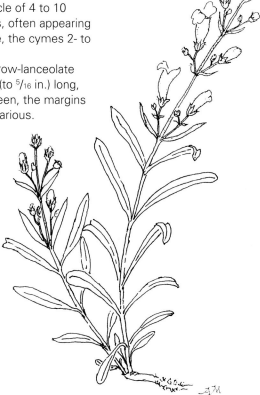

Penstemon kingii

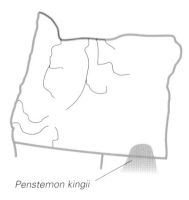

Penstemon kingii

19. *PENSTEMON ROEZLII* REGEL
(*Penstemon laetus* ssp. *roezlii* [Regel] Keck)
Roezl's Penstemon

Penstemon roezlii is named for Benito Roezl, a nineteenth-century plant collector. It has recently been advanced from a subspecies or variety of *Penstemon laetus* to full species status in the Jepson Manual II (Holmgren 1991).

Stems: Several slender stems rising in a clump to 2 to 5 dm (8–20 in.) tall, glandular in the inflorescence, pubescent below, often with sterile leafy shoots at the base.

Leaves: Entire, very finely pubescent and pale gray-green, oblanceolate to narrow lance-shaped on short petioles at the base and on the lower stems, linear to narrowly lanceolate above, commonly folded lengthwise, the blades 2 to 7 cm (1–3 in.) long.

Inflorescence: A mixed raceme above and panicle below, the lower peduncles spreading, of 4 to 12 verticillasters, the cymes loose or open and few-flowered.

Calyx: The sepals linear to narrowly ovate and often dissimilar, acute to acuminate, green or purplish and entire.

Corolla: Bright blue to blue-violet or purplish, the throat lighter, 1.4 to 2.2 cm ($^9/_{16}$–$^7/_8$ in.) long, glandular outside, glabrous inside.

Anthers: Oval in outline and as broad as long, the sacs 1.6 to 2 mm long, purple, dehiscent about $^1/_2$ to $^3/_5$ the length across the connected ends, permanently parallel or horseshoe-shaped, the sutures white-hairy or spiny.

Staminode: White, glabrous, slightly expanded at the tip and just reaching the orifice of the corolla.

Blooming: Late May into July.

Habitat: Dry, rocky or gravelly slopes and flats with sagebrush, juniper or ponderosa pine.

Range: Central Oregon (Wheeler Co.) to sw Oregon, n California in the Sierras and adjacent Nevada.

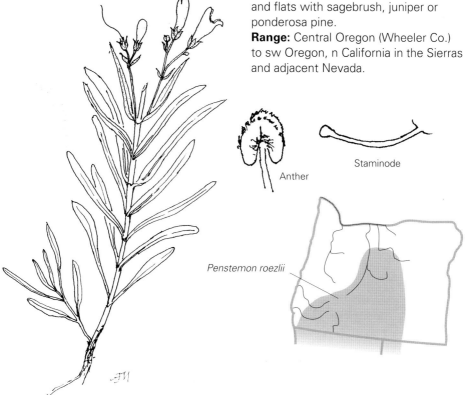

Anther

Staminode

Penstemon roezlii

Penstemon roezlii

20. *PENSTEMON LAETUS* VAR. *SAGITTATUS* KECK
Cheerful Penstemon, Sagittate Penstemon

Laetus means "cheerful, pleasant and bright," while *sagittatus* means "shaped like an arrow," referring to the shape of the anthers. Although *Penstemon roezlii* has been removed from varietal status under *Penstemon laetus,* two more varieties range much farther south in California.

Stems: Few to many, 2 to 8 dm (8–32 in.) tall, slender and lax or sprawling, sometimes turning purple, glabrous or finely pubescent below and densely glandular above.

Leaves: Mostly cauline, but with occasional leafy sterile shoots at the base, gray or yellow-green from a fine, dense pubescence, linear to oblanceolate below, lanceolate and often folded at the midrib above, 2 to 7 cm (1–3 in.) long, the upper leaves sessile and somewhat clasping, all entire.

Inflorescence: Mostly a panicle with 4 to 12 verticillasters but racemose above, the cymes 2- to 4-flowered, the peduncles spreading from the main stem, glandular.

Calyx: Glandular, herbaceous, 5 to 6.5 mm (to 1/4 in.) long, the sepals linear to narrowly ovate, acute and entire.

Corolla: Pink to blue-violet or purple, the tube purple at the base, the lips moderately spreading, 2 to 3.5 cm (7/8–1 3/8 in.) long, glandular outside, glabrous within.

Anthers: Sagittate (arrow-shaped) and appreciably bent or bellied, sometimes almost double, much longer than broad, 1.6 to 2 mm long, white or purple, the sacs dehiscent 3/5 to 4/5 their length, the sutures usually quite spiny-toothed, the longer pair just reaching the orifice.

Staminode: Glabrous and just reaching the orifice.

Blooming: June and July.

Habitat: Sagebrush flats and slopes to conifer forests from low to fairly high elevations.

Range: Southwestern Oregon, Josephine to Klamath Cos., and n California.

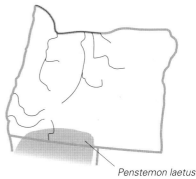

Penstemon laetus var. *sagittatus*

Penstemon laetus var. *sagittatus*

21. *PENSTEMON CUSICKII* GRAY
Cusick's Penstemon

This species is named for William Cusick (1842–1922), a Northwest botanist and prolific plant collector. Keck (1932) theorizes that *Penstemon cusickii* is the progenitor of *P. kingii* and *leonardii* and perhaps many if not all the species in subgenus *Saccanthera* (Group II), although considerable distance separates its range from other species in the subgenus.

Stems: Numerous, slender, brittle stems reach upright in a cluster 1.5 to 4.5 dm (6–18 in.) high from a shrubby base, finely gray-pubescent.

Leaves: Mostly linear to narrowly oblanceolate, all cauline, gray-green pubescent or somewhat glaucous, 2 to 8 cm (³/₄–3¹/₄ in.) long, entire and sessile.

Inflorescence: Narrow and finely nonglandular-pubescent, a mixed raceme at the apex and panicle below, the peduncles of the 2- to 3-flowered cymes press against the main stem and the pedicels of individual flowers are well-developed, of 3 to 10 verticillasters, sometimes congested but more commonly open, the peduncles arising from the axils of leafy bracts below.

Calyx: Of broadly oval sepals, tapered abruptly to acute tips, glabrous or very finely pubescent, 4 to 6 mm long, the margins slightly scarious (white) and entire or slightly ragged.

Corolla: Blue-violet or lavender to purplish, glabrous throughout, 1.5 to 2.4 cm (⁵/₈–1 in.) long, a narrow tube at the base expanding moderately in the throat.

Stamens: The lower pair exserted, the upper pair just reaching the orifice, the anthers mostly glabrous but sparingly pubescent near the connective, horseshoe-shaped, the sacs dehiscing less than ¹/₂ their length across the connective and usually purple.

Staminode: White, glabrous, expanded at the tip and slightly exserted.

Blooming: May into July.

Habitat: Usually with sagebrush on light basaltic substrates.

Range: Southwestern Oregon (Baker to Harney Cos.) and east to Blaine Co., Idaho.

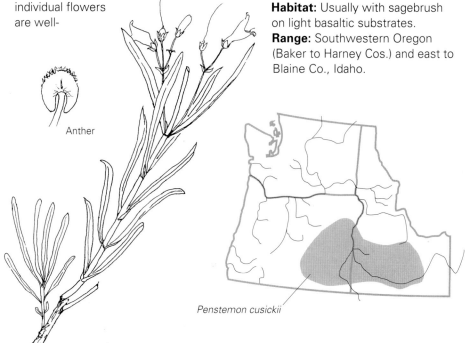

Anther

Penstemon cusickii

Penstemon cusickii

22. *PENSTEMON LEONARDII* RYDB.
Leonard's Penstemon

Penstemon leonardii is named for Fred Leonard (1866–1922), a doctor and plant collector. It occurs quite commonly at subalpine elevations within its limited range in the se corner of Idaho and adjacent Utah.

Stems: Spreading or prostrate at the base and turning up at the ends or bushy, 1 to 3 dm (4–12 in.) long, sparingly branched, with sterile, leafy shoots at the base, glabrous or very finely pubescent.

Leaves: Oblanceolate, tapering more to the base than to the tip, to narrowly elliptic above, 1.5 to 6 cm ($^5/_8$–$2^3/_8$ in.) long, green, glabrous except for minute pubescence on the margins, which are entire.

Inflorescence: 2 to 6 verticillasters more or less crowded as a continuous thyrse, the cymes 2- to 4-flowered, a raceme at the apex, secund and glabrous.

Calyx: The sepals lance-shaped, 3 to 6 mm long, glabrous except for a few sessile glands at the base, narrowly scarious on the margins.

Corolla: Deep blue to violet at the tube (the base), the throat pale to white within, glabrous throughout, the lower lip longer than the upper, the throat shallowly 2-ridged on the palate, 1.4 to 2 cm ($^9/_{16}$–$^3/_4$ in.) long.

Stamens: The longer, lower pair reaching the orifice, the sacs dehiscent only across the connected ends, the suture minutely spiny-toothed, black-purple, glabrous or sparingly short-hairy at the connective.

Staminode: Glabrous, white with a blue, slightly expanded tip.

Blooming: In midsummer.

Habitat: Open rocky slopes or with brush or conifer forests.

Range: The Wasatch Mountains of Franklin and Bear River Cos., se Idaho and south into Utah, sporadic to sw Utah.

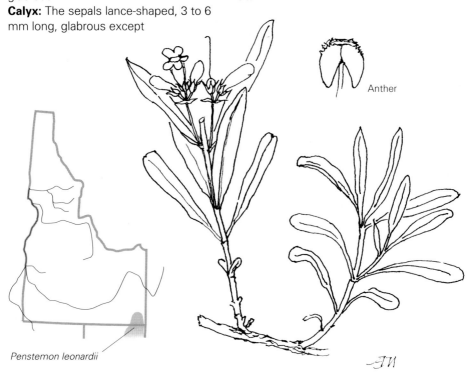

Anther

Penstemon leonardii

Penstemon leonardii

23. *PENSTEMON AZUREUS* BENTH.
Azure Penstemon, Deep Blue Penstemon

This species is obviously named for the deep, rich color of the blossoms. It is essentially glabrous on all parts, although the lower stems may on occasion be minutely pubescent. It is closely related to the smaller *P. parvulus*.

Stems: Normally several stems 2 to 5 dm (8–20 in.) high in a fairly tight cluster from a woody root crown, a subshrub.

Leaves: Mostly cauline, basal leaves 2 to 5 cm (1–2 in.) long to 1.8 cm (³/₄ in.) wide on short petioles, smaller above and sessile to clasping, all leaves with a bluish-glaucous coat.

Inflorescence: Narrow and tight to the stem, secund and normally of several few-flowered verticillasters.

Calyx: The sepals 3.5 to 6 mm (to ¹/₄ in.) long, oblong, abruptly tapered to short, sharp tips.

Corolla: Deep blue or purplish, 2 to 3.5 cm (³/₄–1³/₈ in.) long, the lower lip abruptly reflexed.

Anthers: The sacs dehiscing ¹/₂ to ³/₄ their length across the attached ends, the sutures strongly toothed, 2.2 to 3.3 mm long, the sacs remaining parallel or horseshoe-shaped.

Blooming: In early summer.

Habitat: Open woods and dry slopes.

Range: Southwestern corner of Oregon to n California.

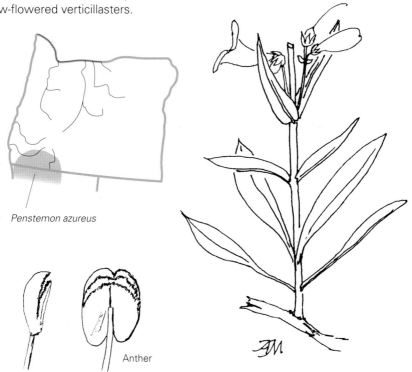

Penstemon azureus

Anther

Penstemon azureus

24. *PENSTEMON PARVULUS* (A. GRAY) KRAUTTER
(*Penstemon azureus* ssp. *parvulus* [Gray] Keck)
Small Azure Penstemon

Penstemon parvulus is closely related to *P. azureus* and was until quite recently ranked as a subspecies of it by some authors. *Parvulus* means "very small." Although it is smaller in stature than *P. azureus,* it is not very small in comparison with several other penstemons. Perhaps its low, spreading nature led to the descriptive Latin name *parvulus.* It sometimes hybridizes with or intergrades into *P. azureus.*

Stems: Woody and branching at the base, spreading to almost prostrate, 1.5 to 3.5 dm (6–14 in.) long, loosely mat-forming, a few sterile shoots at the base, glabrous and somewhat glaucous.

Leaves: Mostly cauline, 1 to 4.5 cm (to 1³/₄ in.) long, narrow to oblanceolate below, lance-shaped to oblong or ovate above, mostly entire, petioled below to clasping above.

Inflorescence: A raceme on smaller plants to panicles on more robust specimens, the cymes 2- to 4-flowered, glabrous, narrow, the lower peduncles closely pressed against the stems.

Calyx: The sepals broad and overlapping, 3 to 5 mm long, variable at the tip, green or purple and mostly entire.

Corolla: Blue to violet, glabrous throughout, 1.4 to 2 cm (⁹/₁₆–³/₄ in.) long.

Anthers: Permanently horseshoe-shaped, the sacs dehiscing ¹/₂ to ³/₄ of their length across the attached ends, with a few short, stiff hairs near the connective, 1.4 to 1.8 mm long with numerous spiny teeth on the sutures.

Staminode: Glabrous or with a few short hairs on the expanded tip and mostly included within the corolla.

Blooming: June into August.

Habitat: Rocky, open foothills to the higher mountain forests.

Range: Siskiyou Mountains of sw Oregon to the high Sierras of central California.

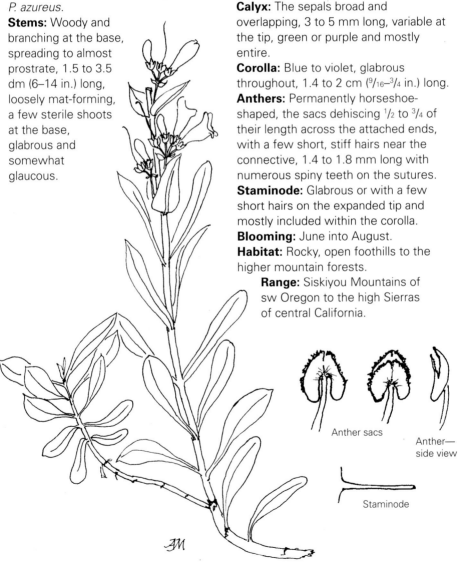

Anther sacs

Anther— side view

Staminode

Penstemon parvulus

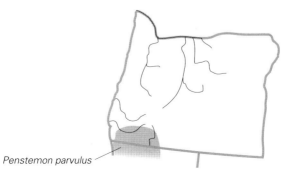

Penstemon parvulus

25. *PENSTEMON EATONII* GRAY
Firecracker Penstemon, Eaton's Penstemon

Penstemon eatonii honors the memory of Alvah A. Eaton, a late nineteenth-century plant collector. Although we have no tall, upright, red- or scarlet-flowered penstemons native to the Pacific Northwest, the Idaho Highway Department has seeded *P. eatonii* together with several other alien species or hybrids along highways in Idaho. It is normally a short-lived perennial and has apparently become naturalized in places in southern Idaho. *P. eatonii*, a species in section *Elmigera* in some floras, has three varieties: var. *exsertus* shows white anthers, noticeably exserted from the corolla; var. *eatonii* is a glabrous plant with included anthers; and var. *undosus* has included anthers and is short-hairy.

Stems: Usually a few rising upright 4 to 10 dm (16–40 in.) tall.

Leaves: All cauline (no basal tufts or rosettes), broadly lanceolate to ovate, 5 to 10 cm (2–4 in.) long, the lower leaves on rather long petioles, the upper leaves sessile to clasping.

Inflorescence: A raceme or few-flowered panicle, composed of 4 to 12 closely spaced verticillasters, glabrous, generally secund.

Calyx: Mostly glabrous, the sepals elliptic to ovate, taper to acute tips, 4 to 6 mm (to $1/4$ in.) long, entire on the margins and narrowly scarious.

Corolla: Bright scarlet, cylindrical and the lips barely spreading, mostly angled downward, glabrous both inside and out, 24 to 30 mm (1–$1 1/4$ in.) long.

Anthers: Short-hairy on the valves, the sacs dehiscing from the outer ends and not across the connective, $1/2$ to $3/4$ their length, the sutures finely toothed.

Staminode: Included within the corolla and glabrous or very lightly bearded.

Blooming: Spring and early summer.

Habitat: Dry open road banks, sagebrush plains to ponderosa pine forests.

Range: Southern Idaho, originally from sw Colorado to New Mexico and s California.

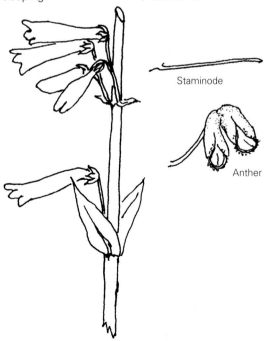

Staminode

Anther

P. eatonii var. *exsertus* (with exserted stamens)

P. eatonii var. *undosus*

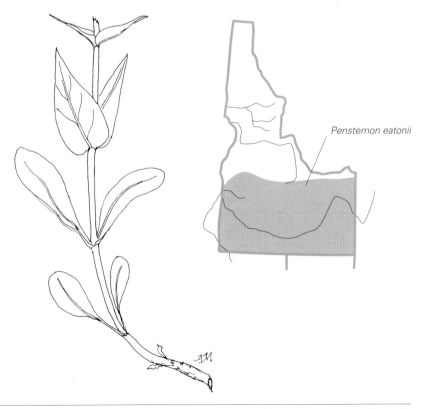

Penstemon eatonii

26. *PENSTEMON IDAHOENSIS* ATWOOD AND WELSH
Idaho Penstemon

Atwood and Welsh first described this small penstemon in 1988. It was first collected and recognized as a new species in 1982. It apparently occurs only on white tuff (volcanic ash) outcrops in one drainage in Cassia County of southern Idaho and adjacent northern Utah and Nevada. White soil particles blown by the wind adhere to sticky surface glands on stems, leaves and flowers, often making the plants fairly glisten.

Stems: Usually several in a low clump, lax at the base, 8 to 20 cm (3–8 in.) long, densely surface-glandular.

Leaves: Linear to oblanceolate at the base, linear to narrowly elliptic above, sessile, 3.5 to 7 cm (1³/₈–2³/₄ in.) long, glistening with sticky glands, the margins entire and curled under.

Inflorescence: Several congested verticillasters, a panicle, the cymes 2- to 5-flowered, secund and densely glandular.

Calyx: The sepals broad at the base taper abruptly to acuminate tips, 5.5 to 8.5 mm (to ⁵/₁₆ in.) long and inconspicuously scarious.

Corolla: Blue to purple, bellied on the lower side, 17 to 21 mm (⁵/₈–³/₄+ in.) long, glabrous inside and out, the petal lobes well-rounded.

Anthers: Purplish and white-bearded, but not hairy enough to obscure the valves, the hairs about equal to the width of the sacs, the sacs spreading at an obtuse angle, dehiscing very narrowly at the outer ends to ⁴/₅ their length, not noticeably toothed on the sutures, mostly included.

Staminode: Bluish, glabrous, included within the corolla.

Blooming: Mostly in June.

Habitat: On white tuffaceous outcrops in dry canyon or sagebrush country.

Range: Cassia Co., Idaho, and immediately adjacent Utah and possibly Nevada.

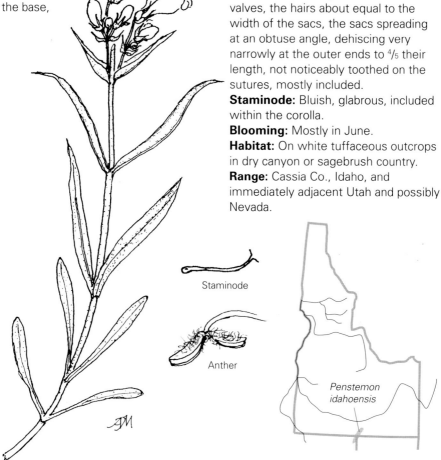

Staminode

Anther

Penstemon idahoensis

Penstemon idahoensis

27. *PENSTEMON CARYI* PENNELL
Cary's Penstemon

Penstemon caryi memorializes botanist Austin Cary (1865–1936), who first collected the species in 1910. Its lovely blue flowers are immediately identifiable by the rather sparse, flexuous pubescence on the anthers of an otherwise glabrous plant.

Stems: A few rise 1 to 3 dm (4–12 in.) tall in a small upright clump, purplish especially above, glabrous and somewhat glaucous.

Leaves: Mostly linear, the lower leaves tapered to a petioled base and sessile above, much-reduced at the base of the plant, 10 to 15 times as long as wide at mid-height, to 7 cm (2$^3/_4$ in.) long, tending to fold at the midrib (channeled) above, glabrous.

Inflorescence: A glabrous panicle, the cymes 2- to 3-flowered, often racemose at the apex, quite crowded, occupying $^1/_2$ to $^1/_3$ of the stem height and secund.

Calyx: The sepals broad at the base, abruptly narrowed to acuminate tips that are $^1/_2$ the length, 5 to 8 mm (to $^5/_{16}$ in.) overall, glabrous, narrowly scarious and sometimes ragged on the margins.

Corolla: Bright blue to lavender in the throat with guide lines, 20 to 25 mm ($^3/_4$–1 in.) long, glabrous inside and out.

Anthers: White hairy overall, the hairs about equaling the width of the sacs, flexuous and not dense, the sacs dehisce about $^7/_8$ of their length from the outer ends, sometimes almost to, but not across, the connective, the sacs 2 to 2.5 mm long and spreading at an obtuse angle.

Staminode: Glabrous or lightly bearded at the broadly expanded tip.

Blooming: Mostly in June.

Habitat: Subalpine forest openings to alpine, more or less rocky slopes.

Range: The Pryor and Bighorn Mts., Carbon Co., Montana, and the Bighorn Mts. of n-central Wyoming.

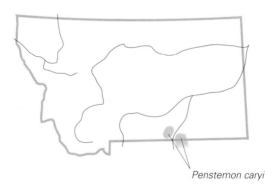

Penstemon caryi

Penstemon caryi

Penstemon caryi

Staminode

Anther

28. *PENSTEMON PAYETTENSIS* NELS. AND MACBR.
Payette Penstemon

This penstemon is named for Payette County or the Payette River and National Forest in Idaho, where it occurs rather commonly and where it was first discovered. Nelson and Macbride first described this smooth, beautiful plant in 1916.

Stems: One or a few stems rise erect in a tight cluster, 1.5 to 7 dm (6–28 in.) tall, glabrous and leafy at the base.

Leaves: Basal leaves large, to 15 or 18 cm (6–7 in.) long including a long slender petiole, the blades mostly ovate; cauline leaves 4 to 8 cm (1 1/2–3+ in.) long, sessile and lanceolate, entire, glabrous.

Inflorescence: A fairly dense, glabrous panicle composed of 3 to 10 crowded or barely separated verticillasters, the cymes 2- to 4-flowered, tending to secund, the peduncles in leafy axils in the lower inflorescence.

Calyx: Lanceolate sepals, acuminate-tapered, narrowly scarious and entire, 4.5 to 8 mm (to 5/16 in.) long.

Corolla: Bright blue to purplish, lighter near the base of the tube, 18 to 28 mm (3/4–1 1/8 in.) long, flaring to a broad throat, the lower lip longer than the upper, glabrous both inside and out.

Anthers: Dehiscing the outer 4/5 or nearly to the connective, the sacs spreading opposite and opening narrowly, just reaching the orifice or slightly exserted, the sutures minutely toothed.

Staminode: Glabrous or sometimes sparsely yellow-bearded and slightly expanded at the tip.

Blooming: Late May into August, mostly June and July.

Habitat: Open slopes and ridge tops to scattered forest or brushy areas from valleys into the mountains.

Range: The Wallowa Mts. of ne Oregon, across central Idaho to the w-central edge of Montana.

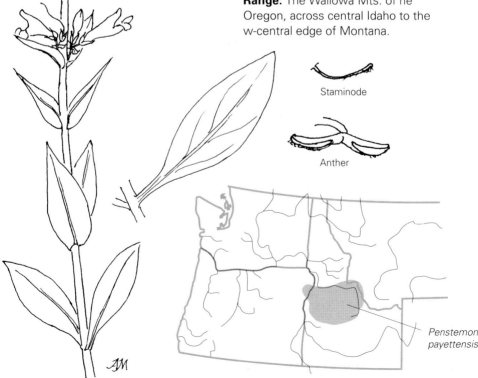

Staminode

Anther

Penstemon payettensis

Penstemon payettensis

29. *PENSTEMON PERPULCHER* A. NELSON
Very Beautiful Penstemon

Perpulcher means "thoroughly beautiful" and this penstemon lives up to its name. It might also be called "stiff stem" penstemon to reflect that property of the plants.

Stems: Few or several stout, rigid stems rise upright 3 to 6 dm (12–24 in.) tall, with some short, nonflowering stems at the base.

Leaves: Narrow, the margins somewhat wavy, glabrous or very finely pubescent, basal leaves narrowed to a petiole, widest near the end, channeled and arched, 5 to 13 cm (2–5 in.) long; cauline leaves reduced upward and sessile.

Inflorescence: Narrow elongate, of 5 to 14 crowded verticillasters, the cymes 2- to 5-flowered, glabrous.

Calyx: Rounded at the base, the sepals tapered to acute tips, 3 to 5 mm (to $^3/_{16}$ in.) long, scarious and often ragged on the margins.

Corolla: Blue to mostly violet, glabrous inside and out, somewhat bellied on the bottom, 18 to 22 mm ($^3/_4$–$^7/_8$ in.) long.

Anthers: Glabrous outside, somewhat twisted or S-shaped, the sacs dehiscing $^4/_5$ of their length or nearly to the connective from the outer end, 1.4 to 1.7 mm long.

Staminode: Included within the corolla and yellow-bearded.

Blooming: Late May and June.

Habitat: Sagebrush plains and hills.

Range: The Snake River Plain of s Idaho.

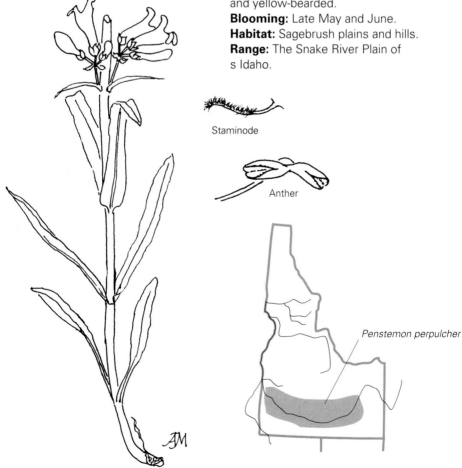

Staminode

Anther

Penstemon perpulcher

Penstemon perpulcher

30. *PENSTEMON SPECIOSUS* DOUGL. EX LINDL.
Royal Penstemon, Showy Penstemon

One of our most widespread and variable species, *Penstemon speciosus* deserves the common name "showy." Different authors have sometimes assigned several varietal names to this short-lived species because of the diversity in its characteristics. However, these variations tend to occur haphazardly or randomly and the segregation into varieties has been dropped for lack of clear-cut distinctions.

Stems: Usually a few stems in a clump, reaching 0.5 to 9 dm (2–36 in.) high, upright or decumbent at the base, glabrous or minutely pubescent.

Leaves: Entire, glabrous or very finely pubescent, basal leaves 5 to 15 cm (2–6 in.) long, narrow to elliptic, on distinct petioles; cauline leaves smaller, linear to lanceolate, sessile, mostly glabrous, flat or channeled.

Inflorescence: Usually long and narrow, of 4 to 12 closely spaced verticillasters, usually somewhat secund, glabrous or sometimes short-pubescent.

Calyx: The sepals lanceolate to ovate, tapered to short, sharp points, 4 to 10 mm (to 3/8 in.) long, broadly scarious and erose on the margins.

Corolla: Bright blue to purplish to violet at the base of the tube, light-colored or white inside, 2-ridged on the palate, more or less deeply incised on the sides forming the two lips, abruptly flaring from the tube to a broad throat, 25 to 38 mm (1–1 1/2 in.) long, somewhat bellied on the floor of the throat, glabrous within and mostly glabrous to rarely glandular without.

Anthers: Reaching the orifice, the sacs dehiscing at the outer 2/3 of their length, distinctly twisted into S-shapes, spreading almost opposite, glabrous externally, very finely toothed on the sutures.

Staminode: Glabrous or sparsely bearded, included within the corolla and slightly expanded at the tip.

Blooming: May to July.

Habitat: Sagebrush prairies to ponderosa pine forest to subalpine.

Range: Central and e Washington to sw Idaho, the Siskiyous of sw Oregon, ne Utah and s California.

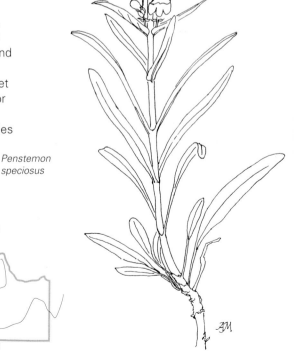

Penstemon speciosus

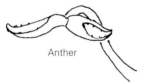

Staminode

Anther

*Penstemon
speciosus*

Penstemon speciosus

31. *PENSTEMON LEMHIENSIS* KECK
Lemhi Penstemon

Lemhi penstemon differs from its close relatives in the length of its calyx and the noticeably channeled leaves, among other characters. It is named for Lemhi County and the Lemhi River Valley in southeastern Idaho, where it was first discovered.

Stems: A few or several stems 3 to 7 dm (12–28 in.) tall, upright, generally covered with very fine, downward pointing hairs.

Leaves: Entire, basal leaves present, 8 to 16 cm (3–6+ in.) long on rather short petioles, narrowly elliptic or oblanceolate, glabrous or mostly finely pubescent; cauline leaves reduced upward, sessile, very narrowly lance-shaped to linear, commonly folded (channeled) at the midrib.

Inflorescence: A narrow panicle, the 5 to 10 verticillasters distinctly spaced over approximately half the stem height, the cymes few- to 10-flowered, the peduncles very short.

Calyx: The sepals ovate at the base, abruptly tapered to a long, narrow caudate tip or acuminate, 7 to 11 mm (to $^{7}/_{16}$ in.) long, strongly scarious-margined and erose.

Corolla: Deep blue-purple on the petal lobes to lavender on the tube, 25 to 30 mm (1–1$^{1}/_{4}$ in.) long, glabrous both inside and out.

Anthers: Pubescent with stiff straight hairs, the sacs spreading nearly opposite and twisted to S-shaped, approximately 2 mm long, the sutures minutely toothed.

Staminode: Glabrous and included within the corolla.

Blooming: June and July.

Habitat: Grassy hills, sometimes with sagebrush from valleys into ponderosa pine forests in the mountains.

Range: East central Idaho and sw Montana.

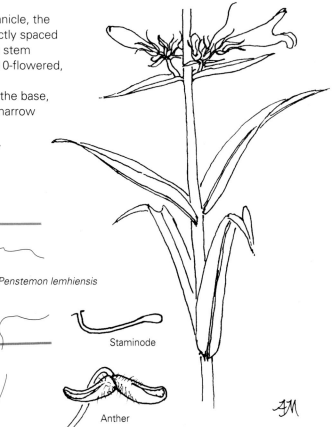

Penstemon lemhiensis

Staminode

Anther

Penstemon lemhiensis

32. *PENSTEMON SUBGLABER* RYDB.
Subglabrous Penstemon

Subglaber means almost, but not quite, smooth or glabrous. Typically the species has a few glands on the upper stem, flowers and sepals. It is closely related to *Penstemon cyananthus* var. *subglaber,* which is glabrous in the inflorescence. The name similarities are unfortunate, but once published are unavoidable according to the rules of botanical nomenclature.

Stems: One or a few reach 2.5 to 7 dm (10–28 in.) high from a thick root crown, glabrous below with a few glandular hairs in the inflorescence, leafy sterile shoots usual at the base.

Leaves: Glabrous and entire, a basal rosette and lower cauline leaves 5 to 10 cm (2–4 in.) long, oblanceolate, sessile or clasping and joined at the base around the stem; upper cauline leaves much smaller and linear to narrowly lance-shaped.

Inflorescence: Narrow with as many as 10 verticillasters distinctly separated, peduncles short, the cymes 1- to 6-flowered and more or less secund, remotely glandular.

Calyx: The sepals lanceolate to ovate, 4.5 to 7.5 mm (to $^5/_{16}$ in.) long, acute at the tip, somewhat glandular and narrowly scarious.

Corolla: Deep blue, the throat whitish inside and the tube shading to violet at the base, glabrous inside and more or less glandular outside, 2 to 3 cm ($^3/_4$–$1^3/_{16}$ in.) long, bellied below and 2-ridged on the palate.

Anthers: Straw-colored, white-pubescent with scattered, stiff hairs, the sacs nearly to completely dehiscent but not across the connective, spreading opposite or even angled upward, 1.5 to 2 mm long.

Staminode: Yellow-bearded in a tuft at the tip, included or slightly exserted.

Blooming: From June into August.

Habitat: Sagebrush plains to brushy openings in canyons and foothills to fir forests.

Range: Southeastern Idaho, sw Wyoming and ne Utah.

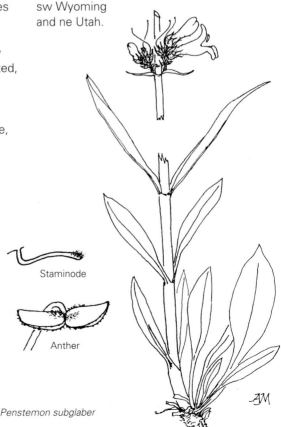

Staminode

Anther

Penstemon subglaber

Penstemon subglaber

33. *PENSTEMON GLABER* VAR. *GLABER* PURSH
Smooth Penstemon, Sawsepal Penstemon

Glaber refers to the smooth, mostly glabrous or non-hairy nature of the plants. *Penstemon glaber* has three varieties, but only var. *glaber* reaches our area in southeastern Montana. The other two varieties range from southern Wyoming to New Mexico.

Stems: One or many stems, upright or, more commonly, decumbent or sprawling at the base, grow 3 to 6.5 dm (12–26 in.) long from a branching, woody root crown; glabrous or finely pubescent.

Leaves: All cauline or with a few short, sterile, leafy shoots at the base, the leaves near the base much smaller than the middle stem leaves, the cauline leaves narrowly to broadly lance-shaped, 3 to 12 cm (1 1/4–4 3/4 in.) long, entire, glabrous or very finely pubescent.

Inflorescence: Glabrous, secund, of 8 to 12 crowded verticillasters, the cymes 2- to 4-flowered, with leafy bracts in the lower inflorescence.

Calyx: Generally 2 to 3 mm long in var. *glaber,* the sepals ovate and rounded or with a short, sharp tip and broadly scarious.

Corolla: Blue to violet, pink or purplish, light blue to white inside, inflated in the throat with guide lines on the palate, glabrous outside and glabrous to white-pubescent on the palate within, 26 to 35 mm (1–1 3/8 in.) long.

Anthers: Short, stiff, scattered pubescence on the outside, the sacs dehiscing nearly to, but not across, the connective, becoming opposite, 1.9 to 2.5 mm long.

Staminode: Glabrous or very sparsely bearded at the rounded, somewhat expanded tip, usually just reaching the orifice or included within the corolla.

Blooming: June and July.

Habitat: The plains, often with sagebrush, to foothills of the mountains.

Range: Southeastern Montana to central Wyoming, sw North Dakota and w Nebraska.

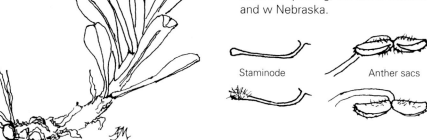

Staminode   Anther sacs

Penstemon glaber var. *glaber*

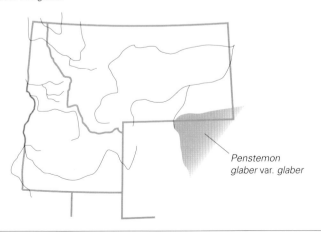

Penstemon glaber var. *glaber*

34. *PENSTEMON COMPACTUS* (KECK) CROSSWH.
(*Penstemon cyananthus* var. *compactus* Keck)
Bear River Penstemon, Compact Penstemon

Penstemon compactus has a close relative in *P. cyananthus* and was considered by Keck to be a subspecies of it. It differs from *P. cyananthus* var. *cyananthus* (but not from *cyananthus* var. *subglaber*) in its relatively narrow leaves and long calyx. *Compactus* refers to the dwarfish, compact nature of the plant.

Stems: Decumbent at the base to upright, a few to several flowering stems and some leafy sterile shoots at the base, glabrous, 1 to 2 dm (4–8 in.) long.

Leaves: Basal leaves robust, 3 to 10 cm (1$^1/_4$–4 in.) long, oblanceolate, tapered to a narrow petiole, glabrous; cauline leaves smaller, lance-shaped, sessile and glabrous.

Inflorescence: A compact, more or less secund thyrse, composed of 2 to 5 crowded verticillasters, glabrous to minutely glandular.

Calyx: Glabrous or sparsely glandular, the sepals lance-shaped or ovate, tapered to sharp tips, 6 to 11 mm (to $^7/_{16}$ in.) long, scarious-margined.

Corolla: Mostly blue to violet on the tube, 18 to 26 mm ($^{11}/_{16}$–1 in.) long, 2-ridged on the palate and bellied below.

Anthers: Pubescent with straight, stiff, white hairs, the sacs dehiscing about $^2/_3$ their length, 1.3 to 1.8 mm long, slightly exserted or included within the corolla, minutely toothed on the sutures.

Staminode: Glabrous or bearded at the tip and included.

Blooming: June to August.

Habitat: On rocky limestone slopes or outcrops, mostly subalpine to alpine.

Range: The Bear River Range in se Idaho and into the Wasatch Range in ne Utah.

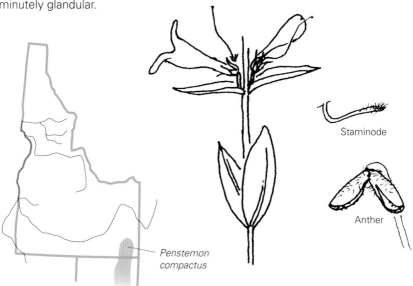

Staminode

Anther

Penstemon compactus

Penstemon compactus

35. *PENSTEMON CYANANTHUS* HOOK.
Wasatch Penstemon, Blue-anthered Penstemon

This species features two varieties: var. *cyananthus,* which has broad lanceolate leaves on the middle stem and broad sepals with short tips; and var. *subglaber,* which bears narrower leaves and the sepals tapered to long tips about half their length. The common name "blue-anthered penstemon" does not always apply, because the anthers on some plants are bright green!

Stems: A single or a few upright stems rise 2 to 7 dm (8–28 in.) tall, glabrous.

Leaves: Basal leaves present, mostly ovate and smaller than the middle stem leaves, tapered to short, winged petioles; cauline leaves narrow or broadly lance-shaped and sessile to heart-shaped and clasping the stem, 4 to 8 cm (1½–3 in.) long.

Inflorescence: Narrow, the peduncles short or long and closely pressed to the main stem when long, of 2 to 8 verticillasters, well-spaced below to crowded above, somewhat secund or surrounding the stem, the cymes 3- to 8-flowered, glabrous.

Calyx: Glabrous; the sepals vary with the variety: ovate with short tip in var. *cyananthus,* narrower with acuminate tip half the length in var. *subglaber;* 3 to 7.5 mm long.

Corolla: Deep blue to lavender or violet, 17 to 25 mm (¾–1 in.) long, moderately expanded in the throat, 2-ridged on the palate and bellied below.

Anthers: Green or dark blue outside, pubescent with scattered, stiff, straight hairs, the sacs 1.3 to 2 mm long, dehiscent approximately ¾ the length from the outer ends, the line of the sutures remaining straight (not twisted).

Staminode: Moderately white- or yellow-bearded and included.

Blooming: Late May to July or early August.

Habitat: Sagebrush flats and foothills to subalpine forest or lower alpine.

Range: Southeastern Idaho, n Utah and w Wyoming; reported from sw Montana, but not confirmed by the author.

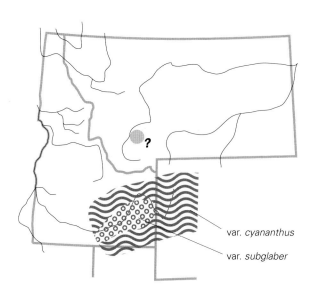

var. *cyananthus*

var. *subglaber*

P. cyananthus var. *cyananthus*

P. cyananthus var. *subglaber*

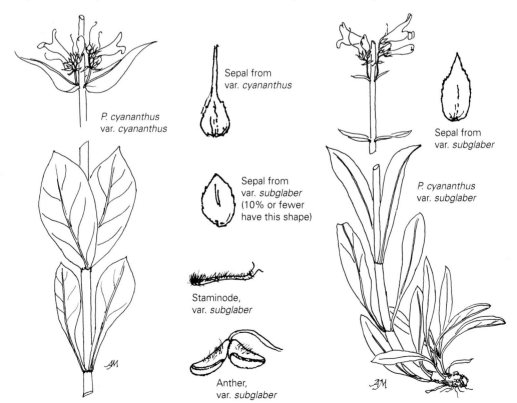

P. cyananthus
var. *cyananthus*

Sepal from
var. *cyananthus*

Sepal from
var. *subglaber*
(10% or fewer
have this shape)

Staminode,
var. *subglaber*

Anther,
var. *subglaber*

Sepal from
var. *subglaber*

P. cyananthus
var. *subglaber*

36. *PENSTEMON CYANEUS* PENNELL
Cyan Penstemon, Dark Blue Penstemon

Cyaneus refers to the dark blue color that gives this gorgeous penstemon its common name. It looks very much like *P. cyananthus* var. *cyananthus* and differs mainly in its twisted, S-shaped anthers. The anther sacs of *P. cyaneus* also are generally longer than those of *P. cyananthus*, but the overlap in size between these two species makes this characteristic an unreliable identifier.

Stems: Usually several stout stems reach 3 to 7 dm (12–28 in.) high from a woody, branching root crown, glabrous and sometimes glaucous.

Leaves: Entire, quite thick, glabrous, basal leaves form a rosette, to 16 cm (6+ in.) long on narrow petioles, elliptic to oblanceolate; cauline leaves reduced, 3 to 11 cm (1–4+ in.) long, lance-shaped, sessile or clasping the stem.

Inflorescence: Glabrous, more or less secund, narrow, of 3 to 10 short-peduncled verticillasters, distinctly spaced or quite crowded, the cymes 2- to 6-flowered.

Calyx: The sepals broad, tapered to acute tips or nearly rounded, 4 to 7 mm long, glabrous, scarious and erose on the edges.

Corolla: Dark blue to violet on the tube, usually light-colored or white within, 24 to 35 mm (1–1²/₅ in.) long, expanded to about 1 cm (³/₈ in.) wide at the mouth, somewhat bellied beneath.

Anthers: Modestly to minutely pubescent with short, stiff hairs, the sacs dehiscent ⁴/₅ their length or almost to but not across the connective, spreading apart at an angle (not directly opposite), distinctly twisted so the anthers are S-shaped, 1.8 to 3 mm long, minutely toothed on the sutures.

Staminode: Bearded with short, yellow hairs, expanded at the tip and included.

Blooming: Late May to early August.

Habitat: Open plains, often with sagebrush, into the lower mountains.

Range: Upper Snake River Plain of s Idaho to sw Montana and nw Wyoming.

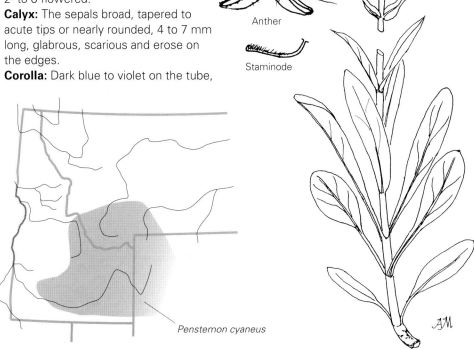

Anther

Staminode

Penstemon cyaneus

Penstemon cyaneus

37. *PENSTEMON PENNELLIANUS* KECK
Blue Mountain Penstemon, Pennell's Penstemon

Penstemon pennellianus honors Francis W. Pennell (1886–1952), a botanist who specialized in the Scrophulariaceae family and genus *Penstemon* at the Philadelphia Academy of Natural Science. The species is closely related to *P. speciosus* and *P. payettensis* and Keck (1940) hypothesized that it developed through hybridization of these two species. The range of *P. pennellianus* approaches those of *speciosus* and *payettensis,* but does not overlap either of them.

Stems: Several stout stems sprout from a branching, woody root crown, 2 to 6 dm (8–24 in.) tall, glabrous.

Leaves: Rather thick, entire, shiny-green-glaucous, the basal leaves large and forming a rosette, 8 to 25 cm (3–10 in.) long, mostly narrow-elliptic and tapered to long petioles; cauline leaves 6 to 9 cm (2$\frac{1}{4}$–3$\frac{1}{2}$ in.) long, reduced on the lower stem to maximum size in the middle, lance-shaped to ovate and acute at the tip, sessile or clasping, the bases of leaf pairs often meeting around the stem.

Inflorescence: A panicle composed of 3 to 10 verticillasters, distinctly spaced in the lower inflorescence to crowded above, the cymes usually 2- to 4-flowered.

Calyx: The sepals lanceolate to ovate and tapered to acute or acuminate tips, 5 to 9 mm long, mostly entire and narrowly scarious on the margins.

Corolla: Blue to purplish, glabrous throughout, 25 to 33 mm (1–1$\frac{5}{16}$ in.) long.

Anthers: Sparsely pubescent with short, straight hairs, mostly near the connective, the sacs dehiscent about $\frac{2}{3}$ of their length from the outer end, not opening widely, the sacs twisted so the anthers are S-shaped, 1.9 to 2.5 mm long.

Staminode: Short-bearded and somewhat expanded at the tip.

Blooming: June and July.

Habitat: Open forest on ridge tops to rocky or gravelly slopes.

Range: The Blue Mountains of se Washington and n Wallowa Co., Oregon.

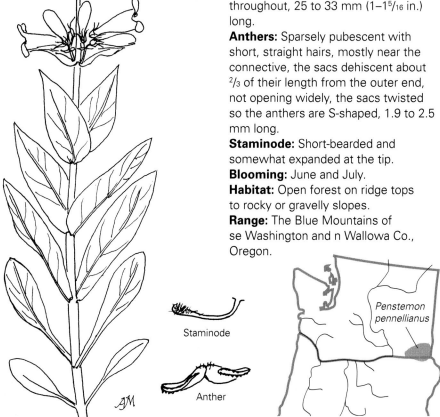

Staminode

Anther

Penstemon pennellianus

Penstemon pennellianus

38. *PENSTEMON DEUSTUS* DOUGL. EX LINDL.
Scorched Penstemon, Hotrock or Scabland Penstemon

Deustus means scorched or burned up. This widespread species is easily recognized, although it varies considerably through four varieties. As shown in the key in this book, var. *variabilis* has some whorled leaves at the nodes, var. *suffrutescens* bears small flowers less than 10 mm long, var. *deustus* has larger flowers with all creamy white petal lobes that may or may not have bright red veins and var. *pedicellatus* shows brownish upper petal lobes. *Penstemon deustus* has two close relatives in northern California, but none in the Northwest.

Stems: Generally forming dense clumps, markedly woody and branching at the base, 2 to 4 dm (8–16 in.) long, usually with many sterile shoots at the base.

Leaves: Variable, mostly toothed, but var. *variabilis* has entire leaves or minutely serrate ones at the outer ends; basal leaves 1.5 to 5 cm (to 2 in.) long on short petioles, glabrous or glandular; cauline leaves sessile or clasping, reduced upward to mere bracts in the upper inflorescence.

Inflorescence: Several to many loose or crowded verticillasters in the axils of upper leaves or bracts, glabrous or sparingly glandular.

Calyx: The sepals 2.5 to 6 mm (to ¼ in.) long, lanceolate to oval, the margins entire and scarious (white).

Corolla: Mostly cream or very pale yellowish, with or without red or purplish guide lines, 8 to 20 mm (⁵⁄₁₆–³⁄₄ in.) long, the tube not much expanded in the throat, the upper lip shorter than the lower.

Anthers: Spreading widely to opposite, the sacs dehiscing flat (explanate), glabrous, 0.5 to 0.9 mm long and mostly included within the corolla.

Staminode: Glabrous or sparsely bearded, not expanded at the tip, usually just reaching the orifice.

Blooming: Late spring and early summer.

Habitat: Dry rocky places or rock cliffs or outcrops from low elevations to subalpine.

Range: Central Washington to sw Montana, nw Wyoming, nw Utah and s California.

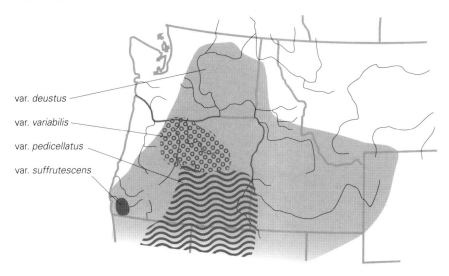

var. *deustus*

var. *variabilis*

var. *pedicellatus*

var. *suffrutescens*

P. deustus var. *variabilis*

P. deustus var. *deustus*

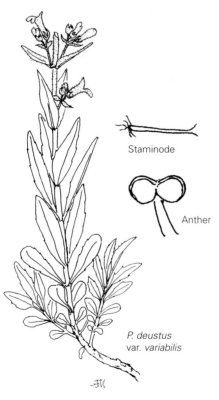

Staminode

Anther

P. deustus
var. *variabilis*

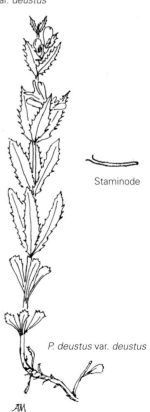

Staminode

P. deustus var. *deustus*

39. *PENSTEMON LARICIFOLIUS* VAR. *LARICIFOLIUS* HOOK AND ARN.
Larchleaf Penstemon

This enchanting little species has one other variety in central Wyoming and the northern edge of Colorado at the base of the Medicine Bow Mountains. Variety *exilifolius* differs only by having white flowers that are also a little shorter. The mat-forming, needle-shaped leaves distinguish the species unmistakably. *Laricifolius* refers to the leaves, which are in clusters (at the base) like those on larch trees.

Stems: A few stems rise from a small, dense mat, 5 to 20 cm (2–8 in.) tall, glabrous or very finely pubescent.

Leaves: Needle-shaped, 15 to 35 mm (^{5}/$_8$–1^3/$_8$ in.) long by about 1 mm wide, forming dense rosettes at the base of the flowering stems, glabrous or finely pubescent.

Inflorescence: An open, few-flowered raceme or panicle, the cymes at most 3-flowered, glabrous.

Calyx: The sepals lanceolate or ovate, tapered abruptly to an acuminate tip, 4 to 6 mm (to ^{1}/$_4$ in.) long, prominently scarious-margined and sometimes slightly erose.

Corolla: Pale pink in our area or slightly lavender to purple in one place in Wyoming, 12 to 18 mm (^{1}/$_2$–^{3}/$_4$ in.) long, funnel-shaped, glabrous outside, the palate finely bearded.

Anthers: Glabrous outside but finely toothed on the sutures, the sacs about 1.3 mm long, mostly spreading opposite and dehiscing to narrow boat shapes.

Staminode: Bearded on the outer ^{1}/$_3$ with short, yellow hairs, sometimes slightly exserted and curved under at the tip.

Blooming: June and July.

Habitat: Dry rocky plains and foothills.

Range: South central Montana around the Pryor Mts. and much of central Wyoming.

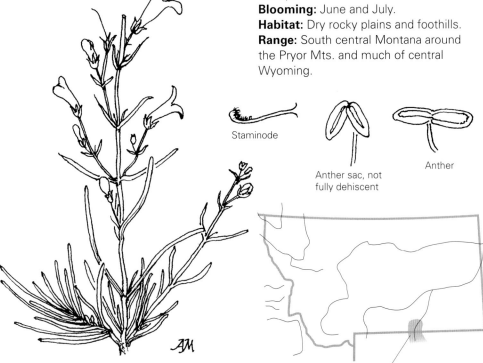

Staminode

Anther sac, not fully dehiscent

Anther

P. *laricifolius*
var. *laricifolius*

Penstemon laricifolius var. *laricifolius*

40. *PENSTEMON ARIDUS* RYDB.
Stiffleaf Penstemon

Aridus means growing in a very dry location. The plants generally form crowded tufts when they are well-developed. Flower color will readily distinguish this species from larch-leaf penstemon, if the leaves are all needle-like.

Stems: Few to many in a tight clump, rising 0.5 to 2.5 dm (2–10 in.) high, glabrous or, more commonly, finely pubescent.

Leaves: Linear and grasslike or narrowly oblanceolate at the base and often folded at the midrib, 1.5 to 6 cm (to 2+ in.) long and 1 to 5 mm wide, glabrous or very finely pubescent; stem leaves narrowly linear to oblong, sessile, the margins finely ciliolate-pubescent.

Inflorescence: Of 1 to 6 loose, few-flowered verticillasters, the lower peduncles pressed tight to the stem, finely glandular.

Calyx: The sepals 2.5 to 5 mm long, broadly oval with white, ragged margins.

Corolla: Blue to purple, pale in the throat, 11 to 18 mm ($^1/_2$–$^3/_4$ in.) long, gradually expanded in the throat, the palate lightly bearded, glandular outside.

Anthers: Glabrous, the sacs dehiscing completely and normally spreading flat (explanate), 0.6 to 0.9 mm long.

Staminode: Yellow-bearded, not much expanded at the tip and just reaching the orifice.

Blooming: Late spring and early summer.

Habitat: Open, often rocky valleys and plains into the mountains, approaching subalpine.

Range: Southwestern Montana and se Idaho to n-central Wyoming.

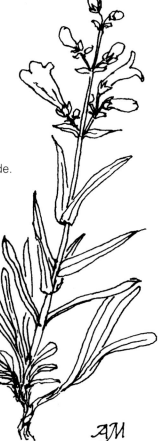

Staminode

Anther

Penstemon aridus

Penstemon aridus

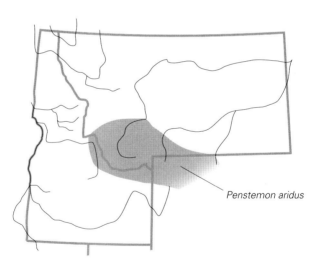

Penstemon aridus

41. *PENSTEMON SEORSUS* (A. NELSON) KECK
Short-lobed Penstemon, Narrow-leaved Penstemon

Penstemon seorsus, considered to be quite rare, is a close relative of the next species, *Penstemon gairdneri.* The petal lobes of *seorsus* are shorter and not as widely reflexed as *gairdneri.* The clasping leaf bases, joined at the base around the stem, perhaps provide a better distinguishing characteristic. In general appearance *P. seorsus* resembles *P. cusickii* much more closely than *P. gairdneri,* but *cusickii* is in a different subgenus—*Saccanthera.*

Stems: Few or numerous, 2 to 3 dm (8–12 in.) tall, grow in a tuft, often with some sterile stems as high as the flowering ones, densely leafy below the inflorescence.

Leaves: All linear, 2 to 5 cm (1–2 in.) long by 1 to 3 mm wide, mostly opposite and clasping, the leaf pairs connected at the base by a ridge around the stem, some leaf pairs may be offset or scattered near the top of the stem, densely fine-hairy and the margins curled inward.

Inflorescence: A raceme or mixed raceme-panicle, few-flowered.

Calyx: The sepals lance-shaped or oval, tapered to acute tips, 3 to 5.5 mm long, entire and narrowly scarious on the margins.

Corolla: Blue to pink but mostly lavender, glabrous inside, glandular outside, 15 to 23 mm ($^5/_8$–$^7/_8$ in.) long, the tube not much expanded, the petal lobes short and not much flared.

Anthers: Glabrous, the sacs dehiscing full length, opening to boat shape and spreading opposite, 0.8 to 1.3 mm long.

Staminode: Yellow-bearded full length, longer than the stamens, exserted from the corolla.

Blooming: Late May and June.

Habitat: Dry, rocky places, often on ridge tops in the plains and foothills, often with sagebrush.

Range: Central Oregon to the sw corner of Idaho.

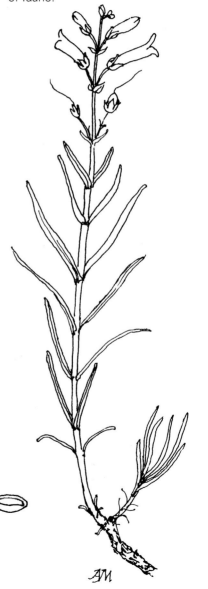

Staminode

Anther

Penstemon seorsus

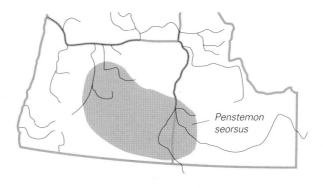

Penstemon
seorsus

42. *PENSTEMON GAIRDNERI* HOOK.
Gairdner's Penstemon

This unusual species honors Meredith Gairdner, an early day plant collector. It is unique among penstemons in being the only species that has truly alternate leaves in variety *gairdneri*. Variety *oreganus,* on the other hand, possesses both opposite and alternate leaves.

Stems: Usually several erect stems rise in a clump 1 to 4 dm (4–16 in.) tall with short, sterile leafy stems at the base, somewhat mat-forming, very finely pubescent.

Leaves: Narrow to linear, entire, numerous, 1 to 7 cm (to 2³/₄ in.) long by 2 or 3 mm wide, not greatly reduced below the inflorescence, alternate or mixed alternate (scattered) and opposite, very finely pubescent throughout.

Inflorescence: A raceme or mixed raceme-panicle, usually from several nodes, few-flowered, the cymes 2-flowered when present, sometimes secund and minutely glandular.

Calyx: The sepals lanceolate to ovate, 3.5 to 10 mm (to ³/₈ in.) long, acute at the tip, entire or slightly erose, scarious and glandular or merely pubescent.

Corolla: Lavender to purple or rose with some white in the throat, the tube not much expanded, petal lobes widely flaring, not strongly 2-lipped, 14 to 22 mm (⁵/₈–⁷/₈ in.) long, sometimes glandular both outside and on the palate, or the palate nonglandular-pubescent.

Anthers: Glabrous, the sacs dehiscent full length, spreading opposite, broadly boat-shaped, usually not explanate, 0.8 to 1.2 mm long.

Staminode: Included or just reaching the throat, bearded on the outer half with yellow hairs.

Blooming: May and June.

Habitat: Dry, often rocky sites, frequently with sagebrush, in the plains to moderate elevations in the mountains.

Range: Central Washington to e Oregon and Valley Co., Idaho.

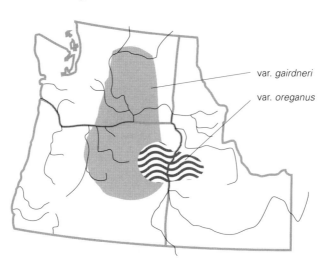

var. *gairdneri*

var. *oreganus*

P. gairdneri var. gairdneri

P. gairdneri var. oreganus

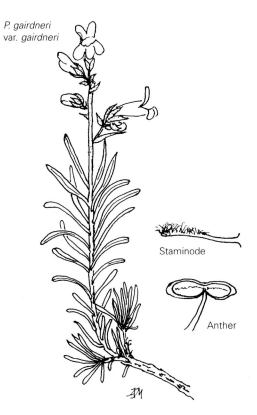

P. gairdneri
var. gairdneri

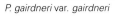

Staminode

Anther

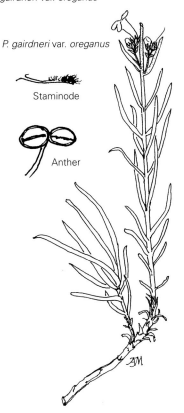

P. gairdneri var. oreganus

Staminode

Anther

43. *PENSTEMON GRACILIS* NUTT.
Slender Beardtongue

Gracilis means "slender" or "thin," referring to the stems or leaves. This species is one of only two of our penstemons in which the root crown branches below the ground, so that the flowering stems die back completely to the ground in winter. The other species is *P. grandiflorus* (see page 114).

Stems: Solitary or as many as four stems, completely herbaceous, reach 1.5 to 6 dm (6–24 in.) high, erect, slender, glandular above, finely pubescent below.

Leaves: Linear to narrowly oblanceolate or elliptic, no basal leaves present, tapered to short petioles on the lower stem, sessile above, 2.5 to 8 cm (1–3 in.) long, glabrous or finely pubescent, light green and thin.

Inflorescence: Narrow, glandular, of 2 to 5 distinct verticillasters, the cymes 2- to 6-flowered, the lower peduncles quite long and held close to the stem.

Calyx: The sepals broad, tapered to short-acuminate tips, glandular, 4 to 7 mm long, entire and sometimes narrowly scarious.

Corolla: Pale lilac to violet, white or very pale inside with strong guide lines, the lower lip longer than the upper and reflexed downward, the upper lip nearly straight in line with the tube, 15 to 23 mm ($^5/_8$–$^7/_8$ in.) long, the tube slender and not much expanded at the throat, glandular outside, white-villous bearded on the palate.

Anthers: Glabrous, the sacs dehiscing full length but not cleaving the connective, opening to narrow boat shape, the sutures finely toothed, spreading opposite, 1 to 1.5 mm long.

Staminode: Bearded with dense, stiff, yellow hairs, commonly exserted and slightly expanded at the tip.

Blooming: Mostly in June.

Habitat: Open prairie, commonly on sandy or gravelly soil.

Range: The Great Plains to intermontane valleys in Montana, n Alberta to Ontario and south to n New Mexico, Wisconsin and Iowa.

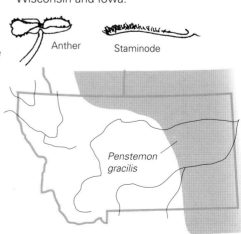

Anther   Staminode

Penstemon gracilis

Penstemon gracilis

44. *PENSTEMON ALBIDUS* NUTT.
White Beardtongue

Penstemon albidus, distinctive because of its white coloration, has the widest range of any *Penstemon* in the Great Plains. The plants are glandular pubescent above with very short, nonglandular hairs on the stems and leaves below.

Stems: Few to solitary, 1.5 to 5 dm (6–20 in.) high, rising from a woody root crown.

Leaves: To 10 cm (4 in.) long at the base including the petiole, reduced above and sessile, lanceolate to elliptic, entire or with small serrate teeth on the margins.

Inflorescence: Of 3 to 9 verticillasters, the cymes 2- to 7-flowered, glandular or finely pubescent.

Calyx: 5 to 8 mm (to 5/16 in.) high, the sepals lanceolate or ovate and acute at the tip, margins entire and often slightly scarious.

Corolla: Creamy white and sometimes tinted pink or lavender, 15 to 20 mm (5/8–3/4 in.) long and glandular-hairy both inside and out.

Anthers: Glabrous, the sacs dehiscing full length and spreading to explanate, 0.7 to 0.9 mm long.

Staminode: Bearded moderately most of its length with yellow hairs, included within the corolla.

Blooming: June and July.

Habitat: Open prairie grassland.

Range: Southeastern Alberta and e Montana to Manitoba, Texas and New Mexico.

Penstemon albidus

Staminode

Anther

Penstemon albidus

45. *PENSTEMON PALMERI* A. GRAY
Palmer's Penstemon, Scented Beardtongue

Named for Ernest Palmer, a botanist, this species is native to the Great Basin and the desert Southwest. It has been seeded for highway beautification in Idaho, especially in the southern part of the state, by the Idaho Highway Department. It differs from all of our native species in the midstem leaf pairs, some of which join at the base to completely enclose the stem. It has apparently become naturalized in Idaho.

Stems: Stout, upright, 5 to 14 dm (20–56 in.) tall, usually a few stems from a thick root crown, glabrous and glaucous.

Leaves: Nearly entire to distinctly toothed, basal and lower cauline leaves ovate and petioled, 6 to 10 cm (to 4 in.) long; some mid- and upper cauline leaves usually joined at broad bases (connate-perfoliate) and others triangular or heart-shaped and clasping the stem, thick and somewhat fleshy, glabrous and glaucous.

Inflorescence: Glandular, of several to numerous verticillasters, the cymes 2- to 4-flowered, secund.

Calyx: 4 to 7 mm long, the sepals broadly ovate, narrowly scarious.

Corolla: Pink to lavender, well-marked with reddish guide lines, 25 to 35 mm (1–1³/₈ in.) long, the tube abruptly inflated to a broad mouth, glandular outside and in, the palate white-bearded, unusually fragrant.

Anthers: Dehiscing completely to broad boat shape, the sacs spreading opposite, 1.8 to 2.2 mm long.

Staminode: Well-exserted out of the corolla, densely bearded on the outer ¹/₃, recurved under at the tip.

Blooming: June and July.

Habitat: Roadsides in dry, open spaces in our area, sagebrush scrub to ponderosa pine forest to the south.

Range: Idaho and the desert Southwest.

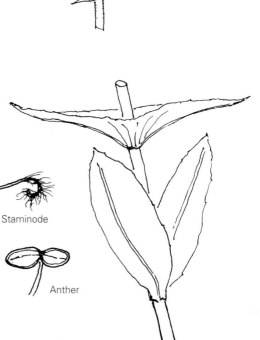

Penstemon
palmeri

Staminode

Anther

Penstemon palmeri

46. *PENSTEMON GRANDIFLORUS* NUTT.
Large-flowered Penstemon, Shell-leaf Penstemon

One of the showiest wildflowers on the Great Plains, *Penstemon grandiflorus* also displays some of the largest flowers in the genus. *Grandiflorus* means "large" or "grand flowers." The waxy, bluish leaves are nearly as attractive as the flowers.

Stems: Only one or two stems originate on an underground root crown, stand erect 5 to 9 dm (20–36 in.) tall, glabrous and glaucous, entirely herbaceous.

Leaves: Petioled at the base and up to 16 cm (6+ in.) long, mostly ovate; cauline leaves nearly round and mostly obtuse on the end, thick and firm, entire, glabrous and waxy-glaucous, sessile to clasping on the upper stem.

Inflorescence: Of 3 to 7 or more distinctly spaced verticillasters, the cymes 2- or 3-flowered, the peduncles very short, racemose at the top.

Calyx: Glabrous and glaucous, 7 to 11 mm (to 7/16 in.) long, the sepals entire and lance-shaped.

Corolla: Pink to lavender or violet with guide lines, glabrous throughout, 3.5 to 5 cm (to 2 in.) long, the tube inflated to a broad oval mouth, distinctly 2-lipped, the petal lobes mostly curled backward.

Anthers: Glabrous, the sacs entirely dehiscent, becoming boat-shaped, spreading to opposite or nearly so, the sutures minutely toothed.

Staminode: Mostly included or just reaching the orifice, bearded with yellow hairs, the tip considerably widened and recurved downward.

Blooming: Late May into July.

Habitat: Open prairie on loam or sandy soil.

Range: Eastern Montana (one location near Miles City) to Minnesota, Missouri and Oklahoma.

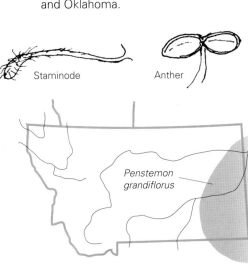

Staminode   Anther

Penstemon
grandiflorus

Penstemon grandiflorus

47. *PENSTEMON ARENICOLA* A. NELSON
Sand Penstemon, Red Desert Penstemon

Penstemon arenicola occurs mainly on the plains of Wyoming, but it may reach into sw Montana according to at least one flora (Dorn 1984). I was unable to confirm its presence in Montana. The name *arenicola* means "dwelling in sand."

Stems: Commonly recline (decumbent) at the base, 8 to 18 cm (3–7 in.) long, glabrous and glaucous.

Leaves: Narrow elliptic, attach mainly to the stem on short petioles below and sessile above, entire, fleshy-succulent and quite glaucous.

Inflorescence: Of 4 to 9 verticillasters, the cymes numerous-flowered, crowded at the top and glabrous.

Calyx: 4 to 6 mm (to ¼ in.) long, the sepals narrow and toothed (erose) on the margins.

Corolla: Violet tube and throat, blue or purplish petal lobes, sparsely bearded on the palate, otherwise glabrous, 12 to 14 mm (½ + in.) long.

Anthers: Glabrous, the sacs totally dehiscent, minutely toothed on the sutures, boat-shaped and spreading opposite, 0.7 to 1 mm long.

Staminode: Golden-bearded and slightly exserted.

Blooming: Mostly in June.

Habitat: Sandy soil of prairies, often with sagebrush.

Range: Central and w Wyoming and reported in sw Montana, nw Colorado and ne Utah.

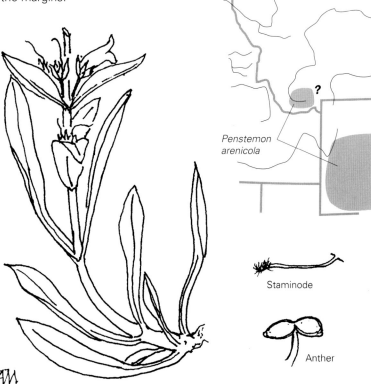

Penstemon arenicola

Staminode

Anther

Penstemon arenicola (photographed in WY)

48. *PENSTEMON ACUMINATUS* DOUGL. EX LINDL.
Sand Dune Penstemon, Sharp-leaved Penstemon

Acuminatus means "tapered to a sharp, acuminate tip" (with concave sides), referring to the tips of the leaves. A short-lived perennial, this species is often easily recognized by the leaves or bracts in the lower inflorescence that are wider than long. However, a race of *acuminatus* in central Washington has leaves that are longer than wide. *Acuminatus* also has two varieties: var. *latebracteatus* has corollas 1 to 1.5 cm (³/₈–⁵/₈ in.) long, and var. *acuminatus* corollas are 1.5 to 2 cm (⁵/₈–³/₄ in.) long.

Stems: One to several; stout, erect, glabrous and quite glaucous; 1.5 to 6 dm (6–24 in.) tall, usually with a few short sterile shoots at the base.

Leaves: Thick and leathery, glabrous and glaucous, entire, basal leaves 4 to 15 cm (to 6 in.) long on stiff petioles, lanceolate or elliptic; cauline leaves 2 to 7 cm (³/₄–2³/₄ in.) long, sessile or clasping, broadly elliptic, abruptly tapered to short, sharp, generally acuminate tips, often wider than long.

Inflorescence: Narrow, elongated, glabrous, composed of 3 to 18 somewhat congested verticillasters attached in the axils of upper stem leaves and bracts, the peduncles short.

Calyx: The sepals lanceolate or ovate and tapered to sharp points, 5 to 9 mm (to ⁵/₁₆ in.) long, green with entire, narrowly scarious margins.

Corolla: Intense blue to lavender or pink, the throat paler and often marked with purple guide lines, the throat moderately inflated, distinctly 2-lipped, petal lobes round and flaring, 1.2 to 2 cm (¹/₂–³/₄ in.) long, the palate glabrous.

Anthers: Glabrous, black outside, the sacs dehisce totally, becoming opposite and shallowly boat-shaped, 0.7 to 1.2 mm long.

Staminode: Glabrous or, more commonly, yellow-bearded at the tip, just reaching the orifice.

Blooming: Early in the season, April to June.

Habitat: Dry, open, sandy places at the lower elevations.

Range: Central Washington to n Oregon, generally near the Columbia River, se Oregon and the Snake River Plain of Idaho.

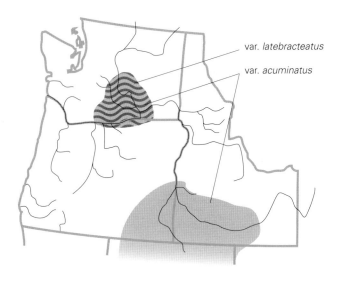

var. *latebracteatus*

var. *acuminatus*

P. acuminatus var. *acuminatus*

P. acuminatus var. *latebracteatus*

Staminode

Anther

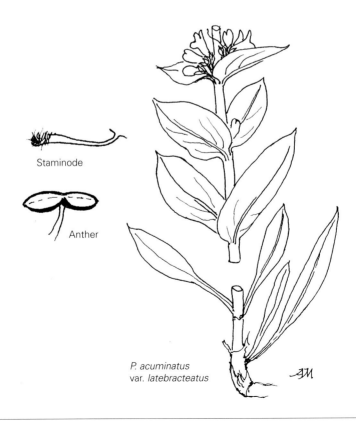

P. acuminatus
var. *latebracteatus*

49. *PENSTEMON ANGUSTIFOLIUS* VAR. *ANGUSTIFOLIUS* NUTT. EX PURSH
Narrowleaf Penstemon, Narrow Beardtongue

Angustifolius refers to the narrow leaves that are characteristic of this variety, but not all varieties of the species. It is usually a rather short-lived perennial and is quite variable through three other varieties east and south of the Northwest. Variety *caudatus* has broader, lanceolate leaves, longer corollas and ranges from Nebraska to Oklahoma and New Mexico. Variety *vernalensis* occurs in the Uinta Basin of Utah and has narrow leaves, while var. *venosus* can be found in s Utah and n Arizona and New Mexico and grows mostly broad leaves.

Stems: One or a few in a clump, glaucous and glabrous or roughened-pubescent, 1.5 to 4.5 dm (6–18 in.) tall.

Leaves: Narrow, some at the base may be a little broader with short, winged petioles, mostly channeled, glabrous and glaucous, 5 to 9 cm (to 3^1/$_2$ in.) long.

Inflorescence: Of 5 to 16 verticillasters usually well-spaced below and crowded above, the flowers encircling the stem, the cymes 4- to 8-flowered on very short peduncles, glabrous.

Calyx: The sepals generally lance-shaped, glabrous and glaucous, 4 to 8 mm (to ^{1}/$_3$ in.) long.

Corolla: Pink to blue, lavender or purple, 14 to 18 mm (^{9}/$_{16}$–^{3}/$_4$ in.) long, glabrous outside, the palate glabrous or with a few hairs, pale inside with guide lines.

Anthers: The sacs dehiscing completely to boat shapes, minute teeth on the sutures, 1.2 to 1.5 mm long.

Staminode: Reaching the orifice, bearded densely with yellow hairs at the widened, recurved tip.

Blooming: May and early June.

Habitat: Open plains to ponderosa pine or juniper woods.

Range: The Great Plains from e Montana and the Dakotas to Colorado, east of the Rocky Mts.

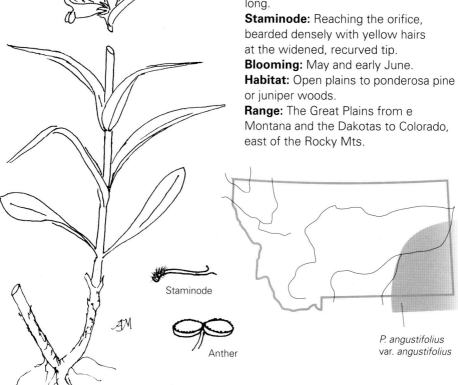

Staminode

Anther

P. angustifolius
var. *angustifolius*

Penstemon angustifolius var. *angustifolius*

50. *PENSTEMON NITIDUS* DOUGL. EX BENTH.
Shining Penstemon

Shining penstemon is one of the more common wildflowers in Montana, especially in eastern Montana. The name *nitidus* means "shining," referring to the shiny glaucous leaves. We have two varieties of *P. nitidus,* separable mainly on the shape of the leaves or bracts in the lower part of the inflorescence. Variety *nitidus* has nearly round bracts, while the bracts of var. *polyphyllus* are narrowly lanceolate. *Polyphyllus* also generally has more crowded inflorescences.

Stems: A few or as many as 7 stems, often curving at the base, 1 to 3 dm (4–12 in.) high, glabrous and glaucous.

Leaves: Broad or narrow, depending upon the variety, basal leaves mostly lance-shaped and tapered to short petioles, thick and leathery, heavily glaucous, glabrous and entire, to 10 cm (4 in.) long; cauline leaves sessile to clasping, lanceolate to broadly heart-shaped or round.

Inflorescence: Cylindrical, of 4 to 10 verticillasters, usually well-separated below but crowded above, the cymes 2- to 5-flowered and glabrous.

Calyx: The sepals lanceolate to ovate, entire and acuminate, glabrous and glaucous, 3 to 8 mm (to $^5/_{16}$ in.) long.

Corolla: Bright blue or occasionally pinkish, often some white showing in the throat with guide lines, the palate glabrous or sparsely bearded, 13 to 18 mm ($^1/_2$–$^{11}/_{16}$ in.) long.

Anthers: Dehiscent completely, opening to broad boat shape, glabrous, the sacs spreading opposite, 0.8 to 1.2 mm long.

Staminode: Shortly exserted out of the corolla, recurved and expanded at the tip, densely bearded with yellow hairs.

Blooming: May to July.

Habitat: Open grassy plains to fairly high elevation in the mountains.

Range: Southern Alberta (also reported from se British Columbia) to s Manitoba, Montana to n Wyoming and North Dakota.

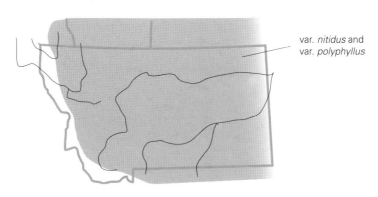

var. *nitidus* and
var. *polyphyllus*

P. nitidus var. *nitidus*

P. nitidus var. *polyphyllus*

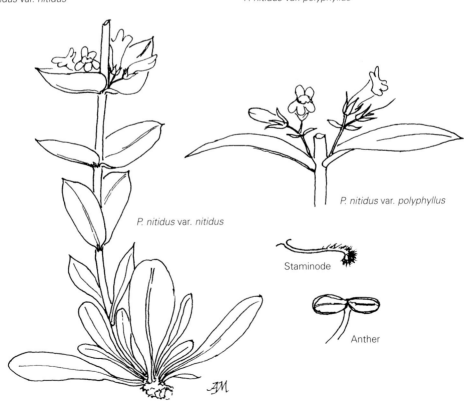

P. nitidus var. *nitidus*

P. nitidus var. *polyphyllus*

Staminode

Anther

51. *PENSTEMON JANISHIAE* N. HOLMGREN
Janish's Penstemon or Beardtongue

Penstemon janishiae is named in honor of Jeanne R. Janish, botanist and well-known botanical illustrator who drew most of the illustrations for the monumental work of Hitchcock et al., *Vascular Plants of the Pacific Northwest*, except Compositae. The long-exserted, bearded staminode and the corolla deeply incised on the sides readily identify this species. It is thought to be closely related to *Penstemon eriantherus*.

Stems: Usually a few stems, erect or decumbent at the base, 8 to 25 cm (3–10 in.) long, create a tufted plant with many short, sterile, leafy stems at the base, pubescent with very short, backward-pointing hairs.

Leaves: Basal leaves 2 to 6 cm (1–2³⁄₈ in.) long on short petioles, oblanceolate, entire or toothed on the outer ends, finely pubescent with backward-pointing hairs like the stems; cauline leaves lanceolate and sessile.

Inflorescence: Of 2 to 5 rather crowded, short-peduncled verticillasters, the cymes mostly 2- to 4-flowered, the blossoms encircling the stems, glandular.

Calyx: The sepals lanceolate, 6 to 10 mm long, glandular and scarious.

Corolla: Abruptly expanded from a narrow tube at the base, bellied below, deeply notched or incised on the sides of the throat forming a wide mouth and two spreading lips, the petal lobes of the lower lip sharply reflexed, pink to purple with distinct guide lines, white- or yellowish-hairy on the palate, 18 to 28 mm (³⁄₄–1¹⁄₈ in.) long and glandular outside.

Anthers: Dehiscing totally, the sacs spreading to almost opposite and explanate, 0.8 to 1.2 mm long, cream to blue and glabrous.

Staminode: Long-exserted, coiled-recurved at the tip, densely bearded nearly full length with yellow-orange hairs.

Blooming: Late spring and early summer.

Habitat: Volcanic soils with sagebrush, scrub or ponderosa pine forest.

Range: Southwestern Idaho and se Oregon, n Nevada and ne California.

Staminode

Anther

Penstemon janishiae

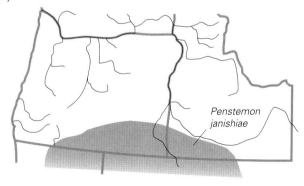

*Penstemon
janishiae*

(Anthers dehisce completely; leaves toothed, some remotely; inflorescence glandular) •

52. *PENSTEMON ERIANTHERUS* PURSH
Crested Beardtongue, Fuzzytongue Penstemon

Eriantherus means "hairy anther," relating to the long-exserted staminode, especially noticeable in var. *eriantherus*. The common name "beardtongue" may well have originated with this species. *Penstemon eriantherus* has five fairly well-defined varieties that may intergrade from one into another on occasion. *P. eriantherus* var. *cleburnei (Penstemon cleburnei* [Jones]) is a Wyoming variety and has not been collected in our area. It very closely approaches south-central Montana, however, and may eventually be discovered in the remote and rugged Bighorn Canyon in Montana. It is the smallest variety and produces entire, instead of toothed, leaves. The four varieties in our area of interest are mostly well separated geographically. For specific differences see the Key to Northwest Penstemons.

Stems: One to several stems reach 1 to 4 dm (4–16 in.) high, sometimes decumbent (curving) at the base and mostly finely pubescent, with short, leafy, sterile stems at the base.

Leaves: Entire or sharply toothed, quite commonly mixed, with some toothed leaves present, narrowly lance-shaped to oblanceolate to nearly linear, glandular or finely pubescent, petioled below to sessile or clasping above.

Inflorescence: A fairly narrow panicle of 3 to 6 well-spaced verticillasters, the cymes 2- to 5-flowered on short peduncles, the blossoms encircling the stems, remotely to densely glandular.

Calyx: 4 to 13 mm (to ½ in.) long, the sepals lanceolate-acuminate, with herbaceous (green) margins and usually strongly glandular.

Corolla: Lavender to blue or purple with dark guide lines, a short, narrow tube at the base expanded to a broad mouth, the petal lobes well-reflexed, 15 to 35 mm (⅝ to 1⅜ in.) long, the palate bearded with long yellow hairs, except in var. *argillosus*.

Anthers: Glabrous, the sacs dehiscent full length, mostly spreading opposite to one another and boat-shaped to explanate.

Staminode: Glabrous or sparsely bearded and included in var. *argillosus* to, more commonly, densely bearded with long, yellow hairs, well-exserted from the corolla and recurved at the tip.

Blooming: Late spring into summer.

Habitat: Dry, open terrain from the prairies into the mountains.

Range: Central Oregon and Washington, s British Columbia and Alberta to North Dakota, Wyoming and n Colorado.

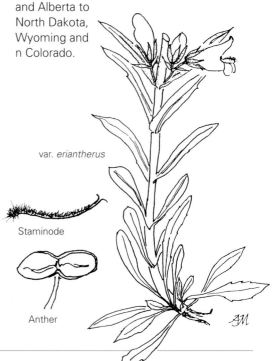

var. *eriantherus*

var. *whitedii*

Anther

Staminode

Anther

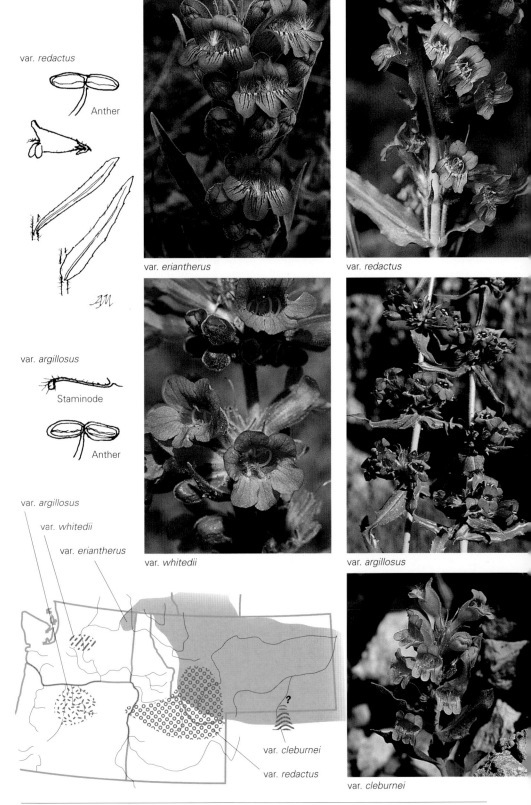

var. *redactus*

Anther

var. *argillosus*

Staminode

Anther

var. *argillosus*

var. *whitedii*

var. *eriantherus*

var. *eriantherus*

var. *redactus*

var. *whitedii*

var. *argillosus*

var. *cleburnei*

var. *redactus*

var. *cleburnei*

(Anthers dehisce completely; leaves toothed, some remotely; inflorescence glandular)   •   **127**

53. *PENSTEMON PRUINOSUS* DOUGL.
Chelan Penstemon, Hoary Penstemon

Pruinosus means gray-pubescent or strongly glaucous, like "hoar frost," referring to the mostly, but variable, densely hairy, often glandular, stems and foliage.

Stems: A few stems usually rise erect in a tuft, 1 to 4 dm (4–16 in.) tall, densely glandular full length or glandular above and gray-pubescent with short, nonglandular hairs below.

Leaves: Mostly broad, ovate to lanceolate on long petioles, $^1/_2$ to $^3/_4$ the length of the blades below, acute-tipped, 7 to 15 cm (to 6 in.) long, finely and sharply toothed, nearly glabrous to glandular or pubescent; cauline leaves to 6 cm ($2^1/_4$ in.) long, sessile, serrate-toothed, lance-shaped to triangular, mostly glandular or pubescent.

Inflorescence: Densely glandular, of 3 to 7 widely spaced verticillasters, narrow, the lower peduncles tightly pressed to the stem, the cymes 5- to 10-flowered.

Calyx: Sometimes purplish, 3 to 6 mm (to $^1/_4$ in.) high, glandular, the sepals entire, acute or acuminate at the tip and narrowly scarious, lanceolate to oblong.

Corolla: Lavender to blue-purple, the throat pale with guide lines, the tube only slightly expanded full length, 10 to 16 mm (to $^5/_8$ in.) long, the lips flaring widely, the lower lip longer than the upper, glandular outside, the palate glabrous or slightly pubescent.

Anthers: Glabrous outside, dehiscent totally, the sacs spreading nearly opposite and broadly boat-shaped to nearly explanate, 0.5 to 0.8 mm long.

Staminode: Usually just reaching the orifice, bearded with a yellow tuft at the tip.

Blooming: May and June.

Habitat: Open sagebrush or pine slopes from canyons and plains into the mountains.

Range: East slope of the Washington Cascades to the central Columbia Basin and north to s-central British Columbia.

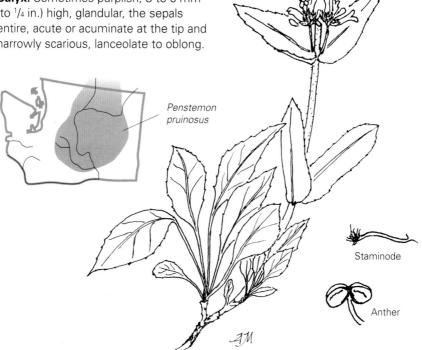

Penstemon pruinosus

Staminode

Anther

Penstemon pruinosus

54. *PENSTEMON ELEGANTULUS* PENNELL
Lonely Penstemon, Elegant Penstemon

Elegantulus means "choice and small or elegant." The species is closely related to *Penstemon albertinus* and could very well be considered a variety of it. The two species differ mainly in the presence or lack of hairs on the stem leaves.

Stems: Few to numerous, slender, 1 to 3 dm (4–12 in.) long, very finely pubescent below the inflorescence.

Leaves: Basal leaves well-developed, 3 to 10 cm (to 4 in.) long including the rather long or short petiole, entire or sparingly toothed, glabrous or, more commonly, finely pubescent, lanceolate or narrowly elliptic; cauline leaves narrowly lance-shaped, sessile, short-hairy, to 5 cm (2 in.) long.

Inflorescence: Of 3 to 5 distinct, few-flowered verticillasters, narrow, the peduncles short and held erect against the stems.

Calyx: The sepals elliptic to oval, acuminate, mostly entire and moderately scarious, 3 to 6 mm high.

Corolla: Blue or blue-violet, the tube gradually expanded, the lower lip longer than the upper, moderately glandular outside, the palate delicately bearded, 15 to 22 mm (^{5}/8–^{7}/8 in.) long.

Anthers: Glabrous, the sacs totally dehiscent, spreading opposite, broadly oval, boat-shaped to explanate, approximately 1 mm long.

Staminode: Mostly included, bearded with a bright yellow tuft of hairs at the tip and somewhat down-curving.

Blooming: May and June.

Habitat: Open grassy ridgetops and upper slopes to scattered timber.

Range: On both sides of Hell's Canyon.

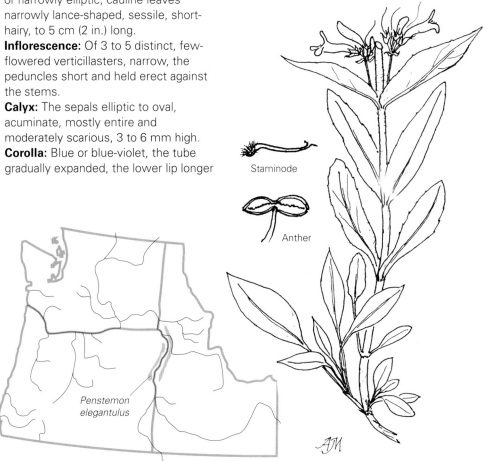

Staminode

Anther

Penstemon elegantulus

Penstemon elegantulus

(Anthers dehisce completely; leaves toothed, some remotely; inflorescence glandular) • **131**

55. *PENSTEMON ALBERTINUS* DOUGL.
Alberta Penstemon

This small to moderately sized penstemon of the northern Rocky Mountains hybridizes freely with *Penstemon wilcoxii* where their ranges overlap and is known to cross with *P. humilis* in southern Idaho. In northwestern Montana most, if not all, plants of the *albertinus-wilcoxii* complex are modified to greater or less degree by interbreeding. These two species differ mainly in the size of the plants and flowers and the spreading of the inflorescence.

Stems: Several stems spreading from the base, 1.5 to 3 dm (6–12 in.) long, from a rosette of basal leaves. Where stems much exceed 3 dm, it is likely the result of hybridization with *P. wilcoxii.*

Leaves: Lanceolate to ovate, the basal leaves to 10 cm (to 4 in.) long including the petiole, sharply toothed to nearly entire, bright green and glabrous; cauline leaves reduced and sessile, more or less finely serrate.

Inflorescence: Narrow to very moderate spreading, glandular hairy and composed of 4 to 8 few-flowered, loose verticillasters.

Calyx: The sepals 3 to 5 mm (to ³/₁₆ in.) long, acute or acuminate, the margins narrowly scarious and mostly entire.

Corolla: Bright blue to pinkish with darker guide lines in the pale throat, the palate lightly bearded, 13 to 20 mm (¹/₂–³/₄ in.) long, the tube moderately expanded at the throat.

Anthers: Glabrous, the sacs dehiscing completely, spreading nearly opposite and explanate, 0.6 to 0.9 mm long.

Staminode: Lightly golden-bearded, recurved and just about reaching the orifice.

Blooming: Late spring to midsummer.

Habitat: Open rocky or gravelly sites from valleys into the mountains.

Range: Southeastern British Columbia and sw Alberta to s Idaho.

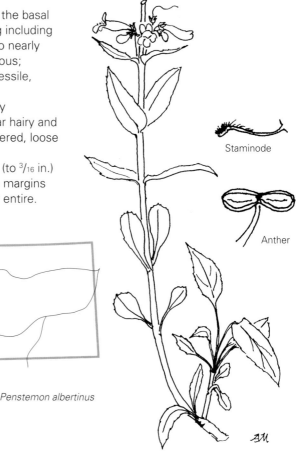

Staminode

Anther

Penstemon albertinus

Penstemon albertinus

(Anthers dehisce completely; leaves toothed, some remotely; inflorescence glandular) • **133**

56. *PENSTEMON ANGUINEUS* EASTW.
Siskiyou Penstemon, Tongue-leaved Penstemon

Siskiyou penstemon is normally very sticky-glandular on the upper leaves and inflorescence, including flowers, stems and sepals, in marked contrast to the glabrous lower stems and leaves. *Anguineus* means "snakelike," which might refer to the flexuous stems on tall plants.

Stems: One to several stems reach 3 to 8 dm (12–32 in.) high from a woody root crown; several sterile, leafy shoots make a basal rosette.

Leaves: Basal leaves lanceolate, 5 to 15 cm (2–6 in.) long, but some ovate to oblong (tongue-leaved), some with fine serrations on the margins; cauline leaves narrowly elliptic or oblong to cordate-clasping, glabrous.

Inflorescence: More or less glandular, of 3 to 10 distinctly spaced verticillasters, the lower ones normally on long, spreading peduncles.

Calyx: 4 to 8 mm (to ⁵/₁₆ in.) long, the sepals entire, acute and narrow.

Corolla: Blue to lavender or purple, 13 to 20 mm (to ³/₄ in.) long, a short, narrow tube at the base and expanded to a broad throat, the upper lip erect and the lower lip spreading.

Anthers: Sparingly pubescent, the sacs barely spreading to opposite and nearly explanate, broadly ovate, 0.8 to 1.1 mm long.

Staminode: Glabrous or sparsely bearded and exserted out of the corolla.

Blooming: Late spring and early summer.

Habitat: Openings in woods, logged areas and road cuts.

Range: Southwestern Oregon, Crater Lake south and west to n California.

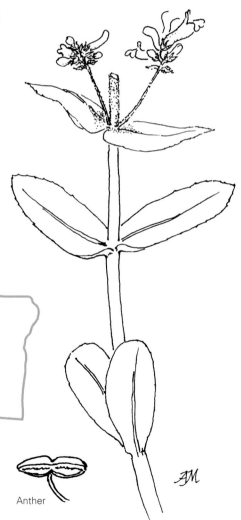

Penstemon anguineus

Staminode   Anther

Penstemon anguineus

(Anthers dehisce completely; leaves toothed, some remotely; inflorescence glandular) •

57. *PENSTEMON WHIPPLEANUS* A. GRAY
Whipple's Penstemon

This species memorializes Amiel W. Whipple (1816–1863), amateur botanist and topographical engineer with the U.S. Army. He was assigned to survey both the northern and southern boundaries of the United States, as well as to plan several railroads. During the Civil War he rose to the rank of major general and commanded a division in the Union Army; he died as a result of wounds he suffered in the battle of Chancellorsville.

Stems: Often only one stem or a few, reaching 2 to 6 dm (8–24 in.) high, upright, may be glabrous or very finely pubescent.

Leaves: Basal leaves well-developed, 4 to 9 cm (1½–3½ in.) long, the petiole half the length, triangular to elliptic-ovate, glabrous, entire or toothed and dark green; cauline leaves to 6 cm (2+ in.) long, sessile or heart-shaped and clasping.

Inflorescence: Glandular, secund, of 2 to 7 rather loose from the stem but crowded verticillasters.

Calyx: 7 to 11 mm (to ⁷/₁₆ in.) high, the sepals lanceolate and acuminate at the tip, entire and mostly herbaceous (green).

Corolla: Two color phases, blue-purple to wine red, or dirty white, cream or greenish (most if not all flowers are cream-colored in the northern part of the range), distinctive with the lower lip much longer than the upper, some blossoms declined, 18 to 28 mm (¹¹/₁₆–1⅛ in.) long, abruptly expanded from a narrow tube at the base, glandular outside, moderately white-bearded on the palate.

Anthers: Blue outside and glabrous, the sacs totally dehiscent, becoming explanate and oval, opposite and slightly exserted, 1 to 1.4 mm long.

Staminode: Bearded with long yellow hairs or occasionally glabrous, somewhat expanded at the tip and exserted from the corolla.

Blooming: July and August.

Habitat: Meadows and rocky, open slopes to scattered timber, subalpine and alpine.

Range: Southwestern Montana, se Idaho and Wyoming to Arizona and Utah.

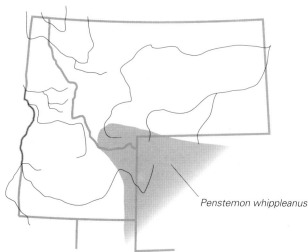

Penstemon whippleanus

Penstemon whippleanus

Penstemon whippleanus (photographed in WY)

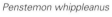
Staminode

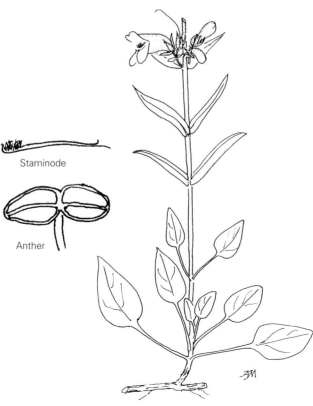

Anther

(Anthers dehisce completely; leaves toothed, some remotely; inflorescence glandular) • **137**

58. *PENSTEMON RATTANII* VAR. *RATTANII* A. GRAY
Rattan's Penstemon

Named in honor of Volney Rattan, this species is closely related to *Penstemon anguineus* and grows quite leggy under a forest canopy. *P. rattanii* var. *kleei* occurs in redwood forests in California.

Stems: Upright or lax, 2.5 to 12 dm (10–48 in.) long, glabrous below the inflorescence, glandular above.

Leaves: Basal leaves shallowly toothed to undulate, 2.5 to 14 cm (1–5½ in.) long with a short, winged petiole, lanceolate to narrowly elliptic, glabrous, thin; leaves mostly cauline, lanceolate, sharply toothed, sessile to clasping above, not much reduced except in the upper inflorescence.

Inflorescence: Of 2 to 7 verticillasters, wide-spreading on long peduncles to branching of robust plants, the cymes 3- to 8-flowered, densely glandular.

Calyx: Glandular, 6 to 9 mm (to ⅜ in.) high, the sepals lanceolate or ovate, acute to acuminate at the tip.

Corolla: Lavender to red-violet, whitish within, abruptly inflated from a narrow tube, strongly two-lipped, the lower lip longer than the upper, glandular outside and moderately hairy on the palate, 2.4 to 3 cm (1–1¼ in.) long.

Anthers: The sacs divergent moderately, not becoming opposite, boat-shaped, glabrous, 1.3 to 1.7 mm long, ovate.

Staminode: Modestly bearded about ½ length with long pale hairs and long-exserted from the corolla.

Blooming: May to August.

Habitat: Woods and grassy slopes to forest openings and margins.

Range: Benton Co., Oregon, south to nw California in the Coast Range.

Staminode

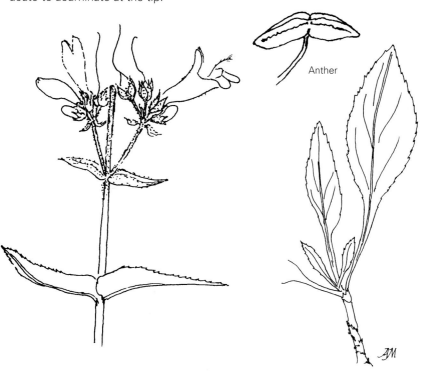
Anther

Penstemon rattanii

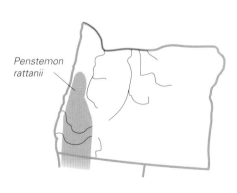

Penstemon
rattanii

Penstemon rattanii

59. *PENSTEMON OVATUS* DOUGL.
Broad-leaved Penstemon

Ovatus means "oval" or "egg-shaped," referring to the broad, ovate leaves. The species is apparently not closely related to any other, but it can be confused with *Penstemon serrulatus* without careful observation of the anthers.

Stems: Few to many in a close, upright tuft, 3 to 10 dm (12–40 in.) tall, leafy below, usually pubescent with short, spreading hairs below the inflorescence.

Leaves: Basal rosette on moderately long petioles, 5 to 15 cm (2–6 in.) total length, markedly serrate, finely hairy or occasionally glabrous, mostly ovate, the lowest stem leaves often oblanceolate; cauline leaves not much smaller below the inflorescence, sessile to cordate-clasping, ovate to triangular, bright green and thin.

Inflorescence: Glandular, fairly narrow to spreading, of 2 to 10 many-flowered verticillasters, the peduncles short or long (quite long when the verticillasters are numerous), moderately spreading away from the stem.

Calyx: 2 to 5 mm (to $^3/_{16}$ in.) long, the sepals ovate to lanceolate, entire and mostly green.

Corolla: Blue or blue-purple, the tube below lighter and expanded moderately, the lower lip much longer than the upper, glandular outside, the palate usually bearded and marked with guide lines.

Anthers: Glabrous, the sacs totally dehiscent and spreading nearly opposite, broadly boat-shaped to nearly explanate.

Staminode: Lightly bearded $^1/_3$ to $^1/_2$ its length with stiff, yellow hairs, recurved at the tip and slightly exserted to just reaching the orifice.

Blooming: May and June.

Habitat: Damp, rocky openings in forests and forest margins at lower elevations.

Range: West of the Cascade Crest, s British Columbia to Multnomah Co., Oregon.

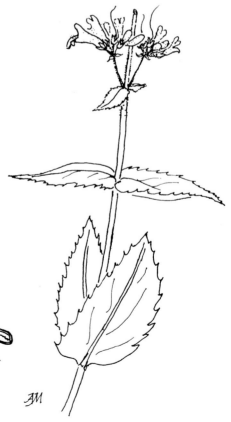

Staminode

Anther

Penstemon ovatus

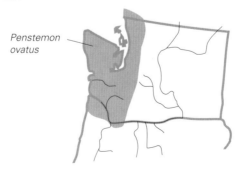

Penstemon
ovatus

(Anthers dehisce completely; leaves toothed, some remotely; inflorescence glandular) •

60. *PENSTEMON WILCOXII* RYDB.
Wilcox's Penstemon

Named for the plant collector Earley V. Wilcox, this complex species assumes several forms. It hybridizes extensively with *Penstemon albertinus* and possibly with *P. attenuatus* and appears to be intermediate between *Penstemon ovatus* and *P. attenuatus*. The inflorescence typically expands broadly with 10 or more blossoms per cyme, but becomes much more compact especially in areas where *Penstemon albertinus* occurs.

Stems: Usually produces several rather slender stems in a clump, 4 to 10 dm (16–40 in.) high, glabrous or very finely pubescent below the inflorescence.

Leaves: Basal leaves variable in shape from elliptic to deltoid, 4 to 20 cm (1½–8 in.) long, petioled about half length, markedly to remotely serrate, glabrous or finely pubescent; cauline leaf blades below the inflorescence often as large as the basal leaves, reduced above, mostly lanceolate to cordate-clasping, strongly to remotely serrate-toothed, essentially glabrous.

Inflorescence: Lightly glandular, a broadly spreading panicle with 10- or more-flowered cymes to narrow and congested with fewer-flowered cymes, especially when transitional to *Penstemon albertinus*.

Calyx: Short, 2.5 to 5 mm (to ³/₁₆ in.) high, the sepals various shapes, often lanceolate, the margins entire to irregularly erose.

Corolla: Bright blue to blue-purple, pale in the throat with guide lines, funnel-shaped, 13 to 23 mm (½–¹⁵/₁₆ in.) long, the palate lightly bearded with yellow hairs, glandular to nearly glabrous outside.

Anthers: Dehisce totally, the sacs spreading nearly opposite, oval and shallowly boat-shaped to explanate, 0.7 to 1 mm long, mostly included.

Staminode: Longer than the fertile stamens, slightly exserted, yellow-bearded and recurved at the tip.

Blooming: May to July.

Habitat: Open rocky sites to fairly thick forest from the valleys and foothills to near subalpine.

Range: Northern Idaho and nw Montana to se Washington, ne Oregon and s Idaho.

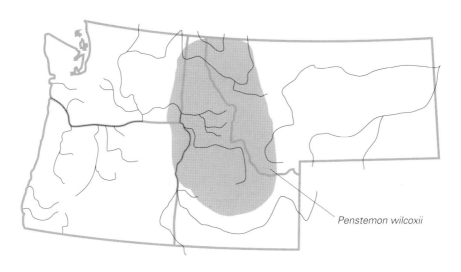

Penstemon wilcoxii

Penstemon wilcoxii

Penstemon wilcoxii X *P. albertinus* (hybrid)

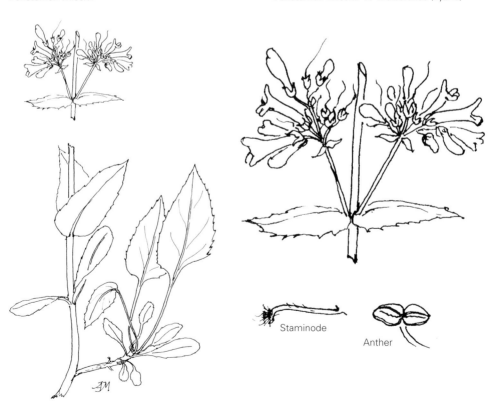

Staminode

Anther

(Anthers dehisce completely; leaves toothed, some remotely; inflorescence glandular) • **143**

61. *PENSTEMON SUBSERRATUS* PENNELL
Fine-toothed Penstemon, Subserrate Penstemon

The name *subserratus* means that the leaves are not quite serrate but finely toothed nevertheless. The species could be mistaken for *P. wilcoxii,* but it is well-separated geographically.

Stems: Many stems normally form a tight cluster 3 to 8 dm (12–32 in.) tall and may be very finely pubescent below the inflorescence.

Leaves: Basal leaves mostly elliptic on long slender petioles, entire to finely and irregularly serrate, 5 to 20 mm (to $^3/_4$ in.) long, glabrous or finely pubescent to remotely glandular; cauline leaves 2 to 6 cm (1–2$^1/_4$ in.) long, lanceolate or narrower, sessile to clasping in the inflorescence, finely toothed.

Inflorescence: Of 3 to 10 well-separated verticillasters, the cymes normally 2- to 4-flowered on relatively long peduncles held quite close to the stems, glandular.

Calyx: 3 to 5 mm high, the sepals oblong to ovate, narrowly scarious and somewhat erose.

Corolla: Bright blue on the tube, paler in the throat, the palate bearded with short yellow hairs, the tube moderately expanded and strongly 2-lipped, lightly glandular outside, 12 to 18 mm ($^1/_2$–$^3/_4$ in.) long.

Anthers: Dehiscent full length, the sacs opposite, shallow boat-shaped to nearly explanate, the sutures sometimes very finely toothed, 0.7 to 1.1 mm long.

Staminode: Reaching the mouth, bearded with yellow hairs and recurved.

Blooming: May into early July.

Habitat: Open woods and clearings.

Range: East slope of the Cascades in Washington to Mt. Hood, Oregon.

Penstemon subserratus

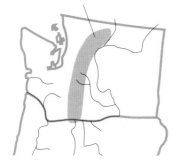

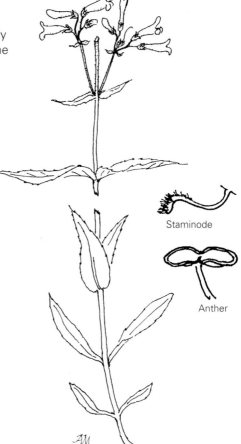

Staminode

Anther

Penstemon subserratus

(Anthers dehisce completely; leaves toothed, some remotely; inflorescence glandular) • 145

62. *PENSTEMON CONFERTUS* DOUGL.
Scorched Penstemon, Yellow Penstemon

Penstemon confertus is closely related to *P. procerus,* as indicated by the crowded thyrse at the top of the inflorescence and the flower clusters that usually have some declined blossoms as well as the small flower size. However, *Penstemon confertus* may hybridize with *P. procerus,* producing pink flowers. The name *confertus* means "crowded" or "dense."

Stems: One or a few stems grow 2 to 5 dm (8–20 in.) tall, often with leafy, sterile shoots at the base or even somewhat mat-forming around the stems, glabrous or very finely pubescent.

Leaves: Entire, bright green and thin, basal leaves in a rosette, mostly elliptical, 3 to 15 cm (1¼–6 in.) long, tapered to short petioles, glabrous; cauline leaves lanceolate, sessile to clasping, to 10 cm (to 4 in.) long, narrow and much reduced in the inflorescence.

Inflorescence: Narrow, encircling the stem, glabrous, of 2 to 10 compact, many-flowered verticillasters or thyrses, the lower flower clusters well-spaced on fairly long peduncles held tightly to the stem.

Calyx: 2 to 5 mm high, the sepals broad with abrupt caudate tips, broadly scarious- (white-) margined and ragged (erose).

Corolla: Cream or pale sulphur yellow, the tube narrow and not much inflated in the throat, but distinctly 2-lipped, 4 to 12 mm (to ½ in.) long.

Anthers: Glabrous and purple outside, the sacs fully dehiscent, opposite and explanate, 0.4 to 0.7 mm long.

Staminode: Included within the corolla, bearded with a tuft of hairs at the expanded tip.

Blooming: From May into August.

Habitat: Fairly good soil or rocky sites from forests to low meadows to subalpine.

Range: Southeastern British Columbia and sw Alberta to the Cascade foothills in Washington, w Montana and ne Oregon.

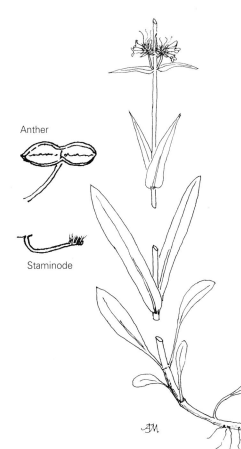

Anther

Staminode

Penstemon confertus

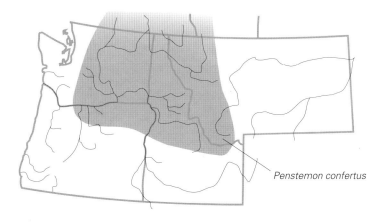

Penstemon confertus

63. *PENSTEMON PRATENSIS* GREENE
White-flowered Penstemon

The name *pratensis* alludes to the habit of this species to grow in rather moist meadows. Because meadows are not common in its range or those that are present have been converted to farmland or pasture, the species does not occur very commonly. *Penstemon pratensis* is quite closely related to *P. rydbergii,* except for its color. It is thought by the author to hybridize with *P. humilis* and it may also hybridize with *P. watsonii,* with which it shares part of its range. The photos opposite were all taken within a few feet of each other in a hybrid swarm in southern Idaho. I found *Penstemon humilis* within flying distance of pollinating insects and assume it to be involved in the hybridization. Also, *P. watsonii,* which occurs in the region, was thought to contribute the very long peduncles on the cymes of some plants.

Stems: Usually several in a clump, glabrous throughout, 2 to 5 dm (8–20 in.) high, with short, sterile, leafy shoots at the base.

Leaves: Narrowly elliptic or lanceolate at the base, tapered to petioles, glabrous, thin and bright green, 3 to 9 cm (1¼–3½ in.) long; cauline leaves much smaller, sessile to clasping above.

Inflorescence: Of 2 to 5 verticillasters, well-spaced below and several-flowered to a dense thyrse at the crown, glabrous.

Calyx: 4 to 7 mm high, the sepals ovate, acuminate or caudate at the tip, broadly scarious and erose.

Corolla: Cream color and sometimes tinted with violet, the tube only modestly inflated at the throat, moderately 2-lipped, 11 to 15 mm (⁷/₁₆–⁵/₈ in.) long, the palate bearded with yellow hairs and 2-ridged.

Anthers: Glabrous, slightly exserted from the corolla, the sacs 0.6 to 0.8 mm long, completely dehiscent, spreading opposite and broadly boat-shaped.

Staminode: As long as the fertile stamens, densely golden-bearded and expanded at the tip.

Blooming: June and July.

Habitat: Meadows and stream banks, high sagebrush valleys to aspen woods.

Range: Southeastern Oregon and sw Idaho to Elko Co., Nevada.

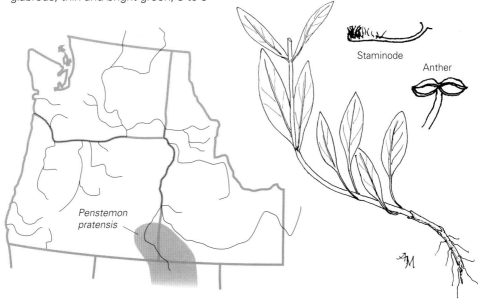

Staminode

Anther

Penstemon
pratensis

*Penstemon
pratensis*

P. pratensis X *humilis* (hybrid)

P. pratensis X *watsonii* (hybrid)

64. *PENSTEMON FLAVESCENS* PENNELL
Pale Yellow Penstemon

Flavescens means "becoming yellow." One near-relative of this species is *P. confertus;* perhaps *P. globosus* is another, but its evolution is the subject of speculation (Keck 1945).

Stems: From a mat or tuft of short, sterile, leafy stems come a few to many flowering stems, 1.5 to 4 dm (6–16 in.) long, commonly decumbent at the base, glabrous or finely hairy.

Leaves: Entire, glabrous, deep green and leathery, the basal leaves 3 to 12 cm (1^1/$_4$–4^3/$_4$ in.) long, a narrow petiole about ^{1}/$_3$ the length, lanceolate to elliptic; cauline leaves mostly oblong to ovate, sessile or clasping in the inflorescence.

Inflorescence: A dense thyrse at the crown and often 1 to 3 fairly dense verticillasters below, glabrous.

Calyx: The sepals ovate or lanceolate, broadly scarious and markedly erose (ragged) on the margins, 5 to 9 mm long.

Corolla: Light yellow or brownish, the tube 12 to 16 mm (^{1}/$_2$–^{5}/$_8$ in.) long and modestly inflated in the throat, the palate yellow-bearded and 2-ridged.

Anthers: Dark purple outside, the sacs dehiscent full length and spreading nearly opposite and boat-shaped, 0.7 to 0.9 mm long.

Staminode: Included within the corolla, bearded with stiff golden hairs at the slightly expanded tip.

Blooming: In the summer.

Habitat: Scattered woods or openings, subalpine to alpine.

Range: The Bitterroot Mts. of w Montana to central Idaho.

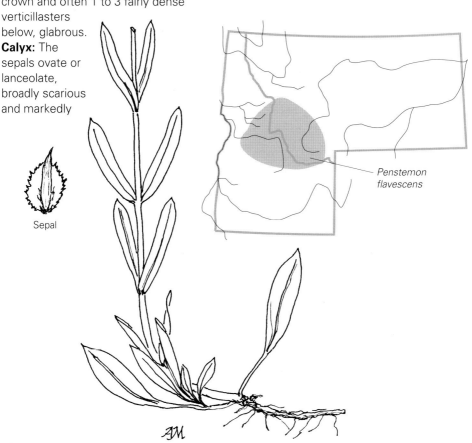

Sepal

Penstemon
flavescens

Penstemon flavescens

65. *PENSTEMON SPATULATUS* PENNELL
Wallowa Mountain Penstemon

Spatulatus means having spatula-shaped leaves. The name has sometimes been misspelled *spathulatus* in the literature. Except for the habitat and range, this species could be mistaken for *Penstemon attenuatus* var. *pseudoprocerus*.

Stems: Decumbent or, more commonly, prostrate, frequently rooting at nodes and mat-forming, 1 to 2.5 dm (4–10 in.) long and branching, finely pubescent, sometimes in lines.

Leaves: Mostly basal, entire, oblong to oval or spatulate, 2 to 6 cm ($3/4$–$2^1/4$ in.) long on well-developed petioles, glabrous and bright green; cauline leaves smaller, narrow, sessile or clasping in the inflorescence.

Inflorescence: Narrow, glandular, of 1 to 4 well-spaced verticillasters, numerous-flowered, the lower cymes on peduncles to 2 cm long held tight to the stems.

Calyx: Glandular, 2.5 to 5 mm long, the sepals lanceolate to ovate and acuminate, mostly entire, narrowly scarious and occasionally slightly erose.

Corolla: Blue to violet, paler within and with dark guide lines, 10 to 13 mm ($3/8$–$1/2$ in.) long, the tube gradually expanded to the throat, the palate lightly bearded, modestly glandular without.

Anthers: Glabrous, the sacs completely dehiscent, spreading opposite and boat-shaped, 0.6 to 0.8 mm long.

Staminode: Densely bearded with stiff yellow hairs, reaching the orifice, the tip not expanded.

Blooming: July and August.

Habitat: Open rocky slopes or with scattered trees, subalpine and alpine.

Range: Endemic to the Wallowa Mts., ne Oregon.

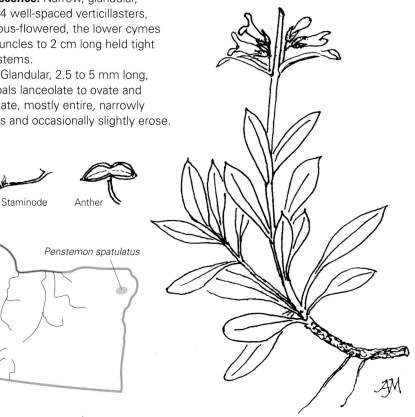

Staminode   Anther

Penstemon spatulatus

Penstemon spatulatus

66. *PENSTEMON RADICOSUS* A. NELSON
Matroot Penstemon

The name *radicosus* refers to the large roots typical of this species. It is quite similar to *Penstemon watsonii* and is thought to be related to *P. gracilis* also, because of the lack of basal leaves.

Stems: Slender, erect, usually a few in a cluster or tuft, 1.5 to 4 dm (6–16 in.) tall, finely pubescent below and glandular in the inflorescence, sometimes with short, sterile shoots at the base.

Leaves: All cauline, entire, the lower leaves short-petioled and reduced, upper leaves sessile, linear to narrowly lance-shaped, glabrous to very finely pubescent, 2 to 6 cm (1–2¼ in.) long.

Inflorescence: A panicle of 2 to 6 distinct verticillasters, the cymes 2- to 5-flowered on fairly long, erect peduncles below, glandular.

Calyx: Glandular, the sepals lanceolate to ovate, entire, narrowly scarious, 5 to 9 mm (to ⅜ in.) long.

Corolla: Dark blue to purple, white within with distinct guide lines, glandular without, moderately bearded on the palate, 16 to 23 mm (⅝–⅞ in.) long.

Anthers: Glabrous, the sacs totally dehiscent, opposite and boat-shaped, often finely toothed on the sutures.

Staminode: Densely bearded ½ length, included within the corolla.

Blooming: May to July.

Habitat: Dry, open areas, often with sagebrush or scattered timber, plains to moderate elevations in the mountains.

Range: Southeastern Idaho and sw Montana to Wyoming, n Colorado, n Utah and n Nevada.

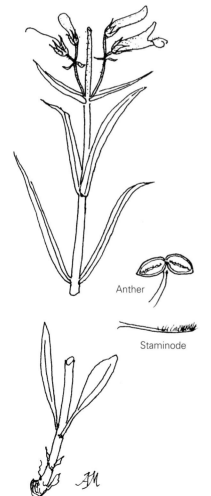

Anther

Staminode

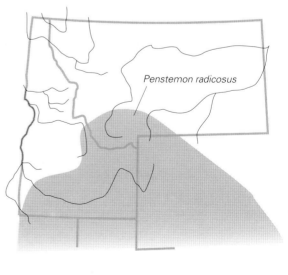

Penstemon radicosus

Penstemon radicosus

67. *PENSTEMON PECKII* PENNELL
Peck's Penstemon

Penstemon peckii honors Morton E. Peck (1871–1958), botanist and author of the *Manual of the Higher Plants of Oregon* (1961). The very small flowers borne by this species relate it to *Penstemon procerus* var. *brachyanthus* and to *Penstemon cinicola,* with which it could easily be confused.

Stems: Long and very slender, 2.5 to 7 dm (10–28 in.) tall, with a few sterile shoots at the base, glandular in the inflorescence and glabrous or very finely pubescent on the lower stem, often red or purple.

Leaves: Nearly all cauline, linear to narrowly elliptic on the middle stem, tapered to winged petioles and reduced on the lower stem, 2 to 5 cm (³/₄–2 in.) long, green and densely fine-pubescent.

Inflorescence: Strongly glandular, open and quite narrow to moderately spreading, of 3 to 10 well-separated verticillasters, the cymes 2- to 6-flowered on fairly long peduncles below, covering ¹/₃ to ¹/₂ of the stem.

Calyx: Glandular, the sepals mostly lanceolate and entire with scarious margins, acute to acuminate at the tip, 2 to 3 mm long.

Corolla: Small, 6 to 10 mm (to ³/₈ in.) long, the tube narrow, the lips modestly spreading (not distinctly 2-lipped), glandular, pale blue to lavender or nearly white, tending to angle downward in the lower inflorescence.

Anthers: Glabrous, the sacs dehiscing completely, nearly round when fully open and explanate, 0.4 to 0.5 mm long.

Staminode: Sparsely bearded with a few short hairs and noticeably expanded on the end.

Blooming: In summer.

Habitat: Dry volcanic soil, usually with ponderosa pine.

Range: Endemic to the east slope and base of the Cascades in Jefferson and Deschutes Cos., Oregon.

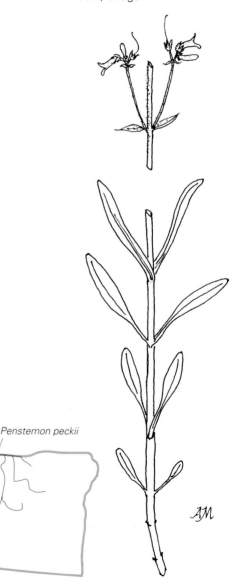

Penstemon peckii

Penstemon peckii

68. *PENSTEMON WASHINGTONENSIS* KECK
Washington Penstemon

Penstemon washingtonensis is endemic to north-central Washington. It is related to *P. procerus* var. *tolmiei* and possibly var. *procerus.*

Stems: Usually several in a tuft, glabrous to finely pubescent in lines, 1 to 2.5 dm (4–10 in.) tall.

Leaves: Basal rosette prominent, 2.5 to 6 cm (1–2+ in.) long including the short petioles, entire, glabrous, dark green, lance-shaped or oblanceolate; cauline leaves few, smaller and sessile, oblong to lanceolate.

Inflorescence: Glandular, a panicle or a thyrse of 1 to 3 verticillasters, crowded and many-flowered, somewhat downward pointing below.

Calyx: The sepals 4 to 6 mm (to $^1/_4$ in.) long, mostly lanceolate with a caudate tip (tail-like), the margins scarious and sometimes erose.

Corolla: Deep blue to occasionally cream-colored, 9 to 12 mm (to $^1/_2$ in.) long, not much inflated at the mouth, lightly glandular outside, the palate well-bearded, the lips only moderately flaring.

Anthers: The sacs completely dehiscent, spreading nearly opposite and broadly boat-shaped or explanate, 0.5 to 0.6 mm long.

Staminode: Included within the corolla, bearded about $^1/_3$ its length with short, stiff, yellow hairs.

Blooming: July into August.

Habitat: Open slopes and meadows at high elevations.

Range: North-central Washington, Chelan and Okanogan Cos.

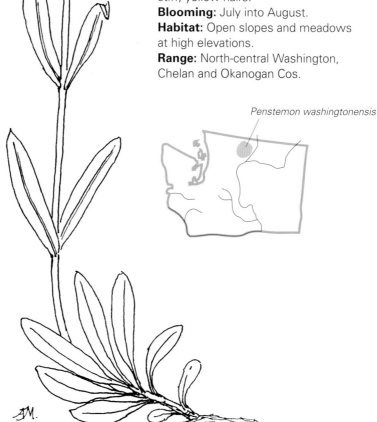

Sepal

Penstemon washingtonensis

Penstemon washingtonensis

69. *PENSTEMON MISER* A. GRAY
Malheur Penstemon, Poverty Penstemon, Golden-tongued Penstemon

The name *miser* means "miserable, pitiable or wretched" and refers to the small size and the ashy gray color of the foliage of this species. Flower size varies considerably. In Malheur County, Oregon, the flowers reach about 15 mm (to $^5/_8$ in.) long, but in adjacent Harney County they grow larger. Farther south in Nevada, the flowers reach their maximum size of 25 to 28 mm (1+ in.), while in northeastern California, they are smallest of all. There does not seem to be any pattern to flower size to warrant segregation into varieties.

Stems: One or a few in a tuft, 1 to 2.5 dm (4–10 in.) high, ashy gray–pubescent, with short, sterile, leafy stems common at the base.

Leaves: Densely ashy gray–pubescent throughout, the shape variable, narrow to broad, thick and leathery, mostly entire but occasional, remote serrations occur, basal leaves 2 to 4.5 cm ($^3/_4$–1$^3/_4$ in.) long; cauline leaves narrowly elliptic to linear, sessile to clasping.

Inflorescence: Narrow, of 3 to 6 verticillasters, the cymes 2- or 3-flowered on very short peduncles, densely glandular, surrounding the stems.

Calyx: Glandular, the sepals variable in size, 5 to 12 mm high, lanceolate and scarious on the margins.

Corolla: Variable in size from 13 to 28 mm ($^1/_2$–1$^1/_8$ in.) long or perhaps more, blue to lavender or purple with dark purple guide lines, the lips strongly reflexed and deeply lobed, the tube moderately expanded at the throat, glandular outside and sparsely white-bearded on the palate.

Anthers: Glabrous, the sacs totally dehiscent, diverging but not becoming opposite, explanate, 0.7 to 1 mm long.

Staminode: Reaching the orifice, densely bearded deep yellow or orange full length, straight.

Blooming: Late May into July.

Habitat: Dry clay soils of volcanic origin commonly with sagebrush or juniper.

Range: Southern Baker Co., Oregon, to central Nevada and ne California.

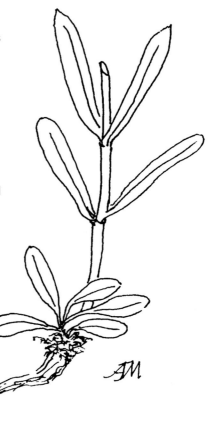

Staminode

Anther

Penstemon miser

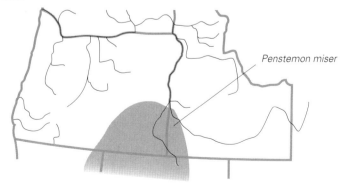

Penstemon miser

70. *PENSTEMON PUMILUS* NUTT.
Dwarf Penstemon

Pumilus means "small or dwarfed." In some places the little plants literally cover the ground in gorgeous massed displays. Unfortunately its range is quite limited.

Stems: Covered with short, backward-pointing, ashy-colored hairs overall and mixed with glandular hairs in the inflorescence, one or several stems prostrate or decumbent at the base, 4 to 12 cm (1½–4¾ in.) long.

Leaves: Mostly in basal rosettes, narrow oblanceolate to linear, 1.5 to 3 cm (to 1+ in.) long, tapered to short petioles, ashy-colored from dense short hairs; cauline leaves the same or smaller, sessile above.

Inflorescence: Few-flowered, a raceme or panicle, the cymes mostly 2-flowered, short and crowded.

Calyx: Pubescent to glandular, 5 to 8 mm (to ⁵/₁₆ in.) high, the sepals lanceolate, herbaceous, entire and mostly acuminate.

Corolla: Blue to purple, turning maroon when dried, 14 to 23 mm (⁹/₁₆–⁷/₈ in.) long, the tube moderately expanded in the throat, sparsely glandular outside and glabrous within and on the palate, sharply 2-lipped.

Anthers: Purple outside, the sacs 0.8 to 1.2 mm long, completely dehiscent and opening to boat-shaped (not explanate).

Staminode: Included or just reaching the mouth, bearded nearly full length with short, bright yellow hairs.

Blooming: From May into July.

Habitat: Dry gravelly places in the valleys.

Range: Salmon River Valley from Salmon, Idaho, to the edge of the Snake River Plain, Lost River to Birch Creek.

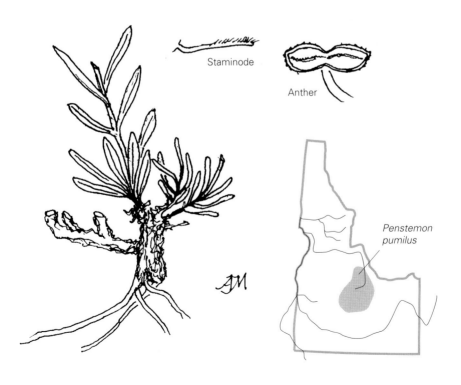

Staminode

Anther

Penstemon pumilus

Penstemon pumilus

71. *PENSTEMON HUMILIS* VAR. *HUMILIS* NUTT. EX GRAY
Low Penstemon, Lowly Penstemon

This wide-ranging species has two varieties outside our area in Utah. At one time it was separated into three other varieties in two species within our range, but when sufficient specimens were available for study, the perceived differences were found to merge one variety into another across adjacent ranges. *Humilis* means "low-growing." It may hybridize with *P. pratensis* (see page 149).

Stems: Few or numerous in a dense clump, 0.5 to 3.5 dm (2–14 in.) high, slender, finely pubescent, with numerous short, sterile stems at the base and somewhat mat-forming.

Leaves: Basal leaves numerous, 2 to 5 cm (1–2 in.) long including short petioles, mostly elliptic, glabrous to ashy-pubescent, entire; cauline leaves smaller, mostly narrow lanceolate, sessile to clasping, mostly gray-green.

Inflorescence: Glandular, narrow, of 2 to 9 few-flowered verticillasters, open below to crowded near the apex.

Calyx: Glandular, the sepals 2.5 to 6 mm (to 1/4 in.) long, broad and tapered to acute tips, narrowly scarious and often purple-tinted.

Corolla: Deep blue to blue-purple, lighter inside with purple guide lines, the tube cylindrical or modestly expanded in the throat, markedly 2-lipped, 1 to 1.7 cm long, glandular outside, the palate white or yellow-bearded.

Anthers: Glabrous and purple outside, the sacs dehiscing full length, diverging and opening to boat-shaped, 0.4 to 0.8 mm long.

Staminode: Included or just reaching the mouth, bearded with a tuft at the tip or 1/3 length with short golden hairs.

Blooming: May into August.

Habitat: Dry rocky plains and foothills to high elevation in the mountains, frequently with sagebrush or scattered timber.

Range: Central Washington, east of the Cascade summit to e California, to central Idaho, w Wyoming and s Utah.

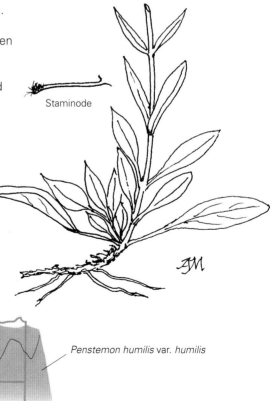

Staminode

Penstemon humilis var. *humilis*

Penstemon humilis var. *humilis*

72. *PENSTEMON GLAUCINUS* PENNELL
Blue-leaved Penstemon

The name *glaucinus* alludes to the waxy, blue-gray, glaucous foliage typical of this species. It is endemic to the Fremont National Forest of southern Oregon.

Stems: A few to many stems grow 1.5 to 3.5 dm (6–14 in.) high in an upright clump, slender and glabrous below.

Leaves: Glaucous, a well-developed rosette at the base, 2 to 6 cm (1–2¼ in.) long including the slender petioles, elliptic to spatulate, mostly rounded on the end and fairly thick; cauline leaves mostly oblong, narrow to linear in the inflorescence, entire, reduced above.

Inflorescence: Of 2 to 4 verticillasters well-separated below to crowded above, narrow, the lower peduncles to 2.5 cm (1 in.) long and tightly appressed to the stems, the cymes 2- to 6-flowered, glandular.

Calyx: 3 to 6 mm long, the sepals mostly lanceolate, the margins entire or remotely erose and scarious.

Corolla: Blue-purple, the tube nearly cylindrical or gradually expanded, 1 to 1.5 cm (³/₈–⁵/₈ in.) long, glandular outside, the palate yellow-bearded and markedly 2-ridged, 2-lipped, the lips spreading but not sharply reflexed.

Anthers: Purple outside, dehiscent full length, the sacs diverging but not opposite, opening to rather narrow boat-shaped, 0.6 to 1 mm long.

Staminode: Included within the corolla, usually glabrous and not expanded at the tip.

Blooming: June and July.

Habitat: In lodgepole or ponderosa pine forests.

Range: Lake and Klamath Cos., Oregon.

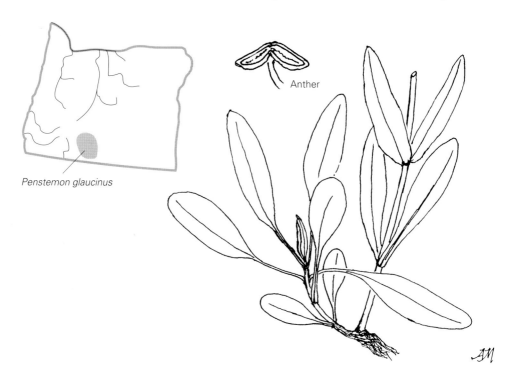

Penstemon glaucinus

Anther

Penstemon glaucinus

73. *PENSTEMON ATTENUATUS* DOUGL.
Taper-leaved Penstemon, Sulphur Penstemon

Wide-ranging *P. attenuatus* is exceedingly variable through four varieties. Further complicating the situation is that where the ranges of two varieties overlap, the two may intergrade one into the other through hybridization. Keck (1945) hypothesized that the four varieties probably had different progenitors, namely: var. *attenuatus* from *P. albertinus* x *confertus,* thus the yellow and pink colorations mixed with blue forms in so-called hybrid swarms; var. *pseudoprocerus* from *P. albertinus* x *procerus,* giving rise to head-like terminal thyrses; var. *militaris* from *albertinus* x *globosus,* thus the source of incompletely dehiscent anther sacs; and var. *palustris,* parentage uncertain, but probably a smaller version of var. *attenuatus. P. wilcoxii* may also be involved in the parentage of var. *attenuatus* and may be responsible for some small teeth on the leaf margins.

Stems: Usually tufted, glandular above and glabrous below or very finely pubescent, 1 to 7 dm (4–28 in.) tall.

Leaves: A rosette at the base, usually on short petioles, mostly lanceolate to ovate, entire, but may be finely toothed in var. *attenuatus,* mostly acute, glabrous to finely pubescent; cauline leaves reduced and bright green.

Inflorescence: Glandular, of 3 to 7 loose or crowded verticillasters, moderately- to many-flowered.

Calyx: 4 to 7 mm long, the sepals entire and usually scarious and acuminate.

Corolla: Mostly 14 to 20 mm ($^5/_8$–$^3/_4$ in.) long, but 7 to 10 mm in var. *palustris,* blue-purple or violet to pink, yellow or white, lightly bearded on the palate, glandular without.

Anthers: Glabrous or very lightly pubescent, the sacs dehisce full length (not quite full length in var. *militaris*), 0.7 to 1.2 mm long, spreading opposite and boat-shaped.

Staminode: Reaching the orifice, yellow-bearded and expanded at the tip.

Blooming: Late spring and early summer.

Habitat: Meadows, piney woods and slopes, low elevation to subalpine.

Range: Central Washington and ne Oregon to w Montana, s Idaho and central Wyoming.

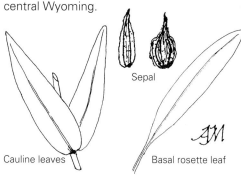

Sepal

Cauline leaves

Basal rosette leaf

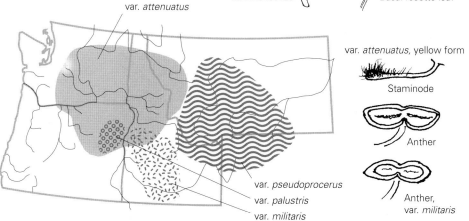

var. *attenuatus*

var. *attenuatus,* yellow form

Staminode

Anther

var. *pseudoprocerus*
var. *palustris*
var. *militaris*

Anther, var. *militaris*

var. *attenuatus* (blue form)

var. *attenuatus* (yellow form)

var. *pseudoprocerus*

var. *militaris*

74. *PENSTEMON PROCERUS* DOUGL.
(*Penstemon tolmiei* Hook.)
Small-flowered Penstemon, Alpine Penstemon

This most wide-ranging of all our Northwest penstemons seems to be misnamed, because *procerus* means "high or very tall." Perhaps the name was given because the species often grows at alpine elevations, but in stature the plants are typically quite small or just average. *Penstemon procerus* has four rather poorly defined varieties, described in this book's key.

Stems: In a tuft or mat-forming, usually with short, sterile, leafy stems at the base, upright, 5 to 40 cm (2–16 in.) tall, slender, glabrous or sometimes pubescent below but not glandular.

Leaves: Basal leaves well-developed or lacking, depending upon the variety, 1 to 6 cm (to 2¼ in.) long on short petioles, entire and glabrous; cauline leaves mostly lanceolate, reduced upward, thin and sessile or clasping.

Inflorescence: Of 1 to several very dense, small-flowered verticillasters, the terminal cluster a thyrse, some flowers typically angled downward, glabrous.

Calyx: 1.5 to 6 mm high, the sepals elliptic to ovate, the tips variable, glabrous or faintly pubescent.

Corolla: Deep blue to purple or occasionally creamy, the tube base sometimes violet, the throat usually light-colored, 6 to 11 mm (to ⁷⁄₁₆ in.) long, the tube not much expanded, glabrous outside, the palate lightly bearded.

Anthers: Glabrous, the sacs completely dehiscent and spreading opposite and explanate.

Staminode: Lightly bearded or sometimes glabrous in var. *formosus,* included within the corolla.

Blooming: May to August, depending on elevation.

Habitat: Dry meadows to open or timbered slopes, foothills to alpine.

Range: Alaska and the Yukon to California, Montana and Colorado.

var. *procerus*

var. *tolmiei*

var. *brachyanthus*

var. *formosus*

P. procerus var. *brachyanthus*

P. procerus var. *procerus*

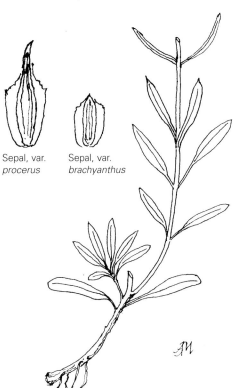

Sepal, var.
procerus

Sepal, var.
brachyanthus

P. procerus X *confertus* (hybrid)

75. *PENSTEMON CINICOLA* KECK
Ash Beardtongue, Ash Penstemon

The name *cinicola* means "dwelling in ash," in reference to its habitat on volcanic ash soils. The species appears to be most closely related to *P. procerus* var. *brachyanthus,* with which it shares its natural range.

Stems: Slender, mostly upright. a few to several growing in a tuft, 1.5 to 4 dm (6–16 in.) tall, often with short, sterile leafy shoots at the base, glabrous or very finely pubescent.

Leaves: Linear, entire, glabrous to minutely pubescent, often arched and channeled, basal rosette lacking, 2.5 to 6 cm (1–2+ in.) long, not much reduced upward below the upper inflorescence, tapered to very slender petioles on the lower stem.

Inflorescence: Narrow, of 3 to 7 many-flowered verticillasters, well-spaced below to crowded above, the lower peduncles on robust plants to 5.5 cm (2+ in.) long, held tightly against the stems, mostly glabrous to finely pubescent.

Calyx: The sepals mostly broad at the base and abruptly truncate with a short, sharp tip (mucronate),1.5 to 2.5 mm long, broadly scarious and often erose on the margins.

Corolla: Dark blue to purple, lighter or white in the throat, 5 to 10 mm (³/₁₆–³/₈ in.) long, the tube not much expanded, the 2-ridged palate moderately to strongly tufted with yellow hairs, 2-lipped, the lower lip nearly straight, the upper lip reflexed.

Anthers: Glabrous, the sacs rotund, explanate and opposite, 0.3 to 0.5 mm long.

Staminode: Included, expanded at the tip and bearded very moderately with short yellow hairs.

Blooming: June and July.

Habitat: Dry rocky to sandy volcanic soils in openings in the forests with sagebrush.

Range: East base of the Cascades in Deschutes and w Crook Cos. to Lake Co., Oregon, to n California.

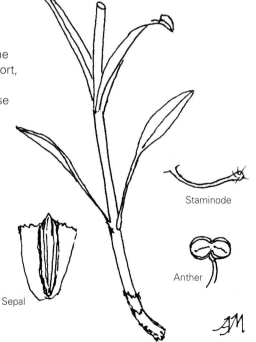

Penstemon cinicola

Staminode

Anther

Sepal

Penstemon cinicola

76. *PENSTEMON LAXUS* A. NELSON
Loose Penstemon, Lax Penstemon

A dense tuft of hairs completely filling the throat of the corolla quickly identifies this unusual species. The name *laxus* means "loose" or in an open arrangement. What the first collector, Aven Nelson, had in mind in naming this species is rather obscure, but he may have meant to describe the rather wide spacing of plants and stems in the typical colony of the species. *Penstemon laxus* is thought to be closely related to *Penstemon watsonii,* but the ranges of the two species are separated by the Snake River Plain in southern Idaho.

Stems: Usually one or few, slender, 3 to 7 dm (12–28 in.) tall, very remotely hairy below to glabrous above.

Leaves: All cauline, small and withering at the base of the stems, narrowly lanceolate to linear, 4 to 9 cm (1¹/₂–3¹/₂ in.) long, sessile and mostly glabrous, entire.

Inflorescence: 1 to mostly 3 to 5 verticillasters, the two or three at the crown very dense, the lower ones if present well-separated and on peduncles to 3 cm (1+ in.) long and tightly pressed against the stem, the cymes mostly 6- to 10-flowered, glandular.

Calyx: The sepals mostly truncate with short, sharp tips or acute, 2 to 3.5 mm long, scarious and sometimes erose.

Corolla: Blue or blue-purple; a dense tuft of hairs on the palate occludes the throat; the tube narrow and slightly bellied below, 11 to 15 mm (⁷/₁₆–⁵/₈ in.) long, glabrous outside and many angled downward.

Anthers: Glabrous, the sacs completely dehiscent, opposite and broadly boat-shaped to nearly explanate.

Staminode: Included and glabrous to bearded.

Blooming: June and July.

Habitat: Dry meadows and open or wooded slopes from the foothills into the mountains.

Range: Southwest and s-central Idaho, north of the Snake River Plain.

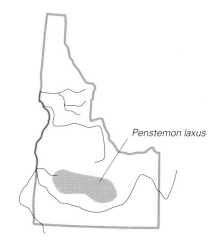

Penstemon laxus

Penstemon laxus

Penstemon laxus

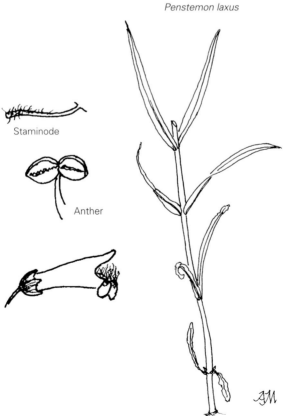

Staminode

Anther

77. *PENSTEMON WATSONII* A. GRAY
Watson's Penstemon

This species honors Sereno Watson (1826–1892), Western explorer and botanist. It is thought to be closely related to *Penstemon laxus*.

Stems: Usually several in a clump, 2.5 to 6 dm (10–24 in.) high, upright, glabrous to remotely pubescent.

Leaves: All cauline, small and withering near the base, mostly narrow lanceolate and sessile, 3 to 7 cm (1$\frac{1}{4}$–2$\frac{3}{4}$ in.) long, glabrous or pubescent, entire.

Inflorescence: Glabrous to finely pubescent, not glandular, of 2 to 6 loose and relatively few-flowered verticillasters, encircling the stem.

Calyx: The sepals oval, 1.8 to 3 mm (to $\frac{1}{8}$ in.) long, obtuse or acute at the tip, slightly scarious on the margins.

Corolla: Violet on the tube at the base to blue on the limb and petal lobes, cylindrical to moderately expanded at the mouth, 12 to 16 mm ($\frac{1}{2}$–$\frac{5}{8}$ in.) long, glabrous outside, the palate moderately white-bearded.

Anthers: The sacs glabrous, dehiscent full length, spreading to boat-shaped, 0.9 to 1 mm long.

Staminode: Included within the corolla, densely bearded about $\frac{2}{3}$ its length and moderately recurved.

Blooming: Late spring and early summer.

Habitat: Gravelly or rocky hillsides with sagebrush or scrub, sometimes including limber pine.

Range: Southern Idaho to central Nevada, sw Wyoming and nw Colorado.

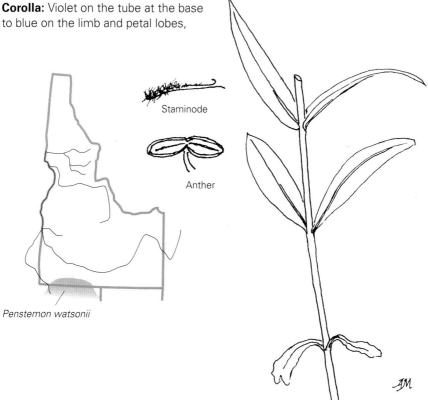

Staminode

Anther

Penstemon watsonii

Penstemon watsonii

78. *PENSTEMON GLOBOSUS* PENNELL AND KECK
Globe Penstemon

The outstanding feature of this species is the globe-shaped thyrse, the dense head of relatively large flowers at the crest of each stem. The anthers, which commonly do not open full length, leaving a slight pouch at one or both ends, also readily identify *Penstemon globosus*. It is perhaps the most beautiful species related to *P. procerus*. On favorable sites the plants may form tight colonies of breathtaking beauty.

Stems: Several to many stems grow in a clump on each plant, 2 to 6 dm (8–24 in.) high, slender to stout, mostly glabrous but sometimes faintly pubescent in lines.

Leaves: Basal leaves profuse in well-developed rosettes, 5 to 18 cm (2–7¼ in.) long on slender petioles up to half the length, lanceolate to elliptic, entire and glabrous; cauline leaves not much smaller below the inflorescence, lanceolate to oblong, sessile and often clasping, thin and bright green.

Inflorescence: A dense capitate head or thyrse at the crown, sometimes with 1 to 3 well-separated, many-flowered verticillasters below, the lower ones on peduncles to 5 cm (2 in.) long held tightly to the stem.

Calyx: 5 to 8 mm (to ⁵/₁₆ in.) high, the sepals broad, often strongly scarious and erose on the margins.

Corolla: Funnel-shaped to a broad, oval mouth, 15 to 20 mm (⁵/₈–³/₄ in.) long, glabrous, bright blue or blue-purple, the palate ridged and yellow-bearded.

Anthers: Glabrous, the sacs commonly dehiscent not quite full length, usually from the connective to ⁴/₅ or ⁷/₈ of the length, leaving a slight pouch on the outer end, minutely toothed on the sutures, 0.7 to 1.2 mm long.

Staminode: Included, bearded about half length with yellow hairs.

Blooming: June to August.

Habitat: Wet or dry meadows in the mountains, moderate to high elevations.

Range: Wallowa Mts., ne Oregon, central Idaho to the edge of Montana.

Staminode

Anther

Penstemon globosus

Penstemon globosus

79. *PENSTEMON EUGLAUCUS* ENGLISH
Glaucous Penstemon

This one is very similar to *Penstemon rydbergii* except that the foliage is glabrous and very glaucous throughout. *Euglaucus* indicates very blue-glaucous or somewhat waxy leaves.

Stems: Usually several slender stems grow in a tuft, 1.5 to 6 dm (6–24 in.) tall with some short, sterile, leafy stems at the base, glabrous.

Leaves: Glaucous, glabrous and entire, the basal leaves elliptic and abundant, tapered to slender petioles at the base, 2.5 to 10 cm (1–4 in.) long; cauline leaves oblanceolate and small near the base, narrow elliptic to linear above, sessile, the nodes typically few and widely spaced above.

Inflorescence: Of 2 to 4 few-flowered verticillasters, well-separated, the cymes mostly 2- to 4-flowered, the lowermost on peduncles 2 to 2.5 cm (to 1 in.) long, held tightly to the stem.

Calyx: 3.5 to 5 mm long, the sepals oval and tapered abruptly to sharp narrow tips, broadly scarious and erose.

Corolla: Dark blue to lavender, white in the throat, the tube moderately inflated, the lips reflexed, 11 to 15 mm ($^7/_{16}$–$^5/_8$ in.) long, the palate 2-ridged and lightly bearded on the ridges.

Anthers: The sacs boat-shaped, dehiscing totally or just not quite completely (reportedly), spreading nearly opposite, 0.5 to 0.7 mm long.

Staminode: Usually just reaching the orifice, bearded with short yellow hairs.

Blooming: July and August.

Habitat: Dry, sandy, volcanic ash soils, open or sparsely wooded slopes from moderate to high elevations.

Range: The Cascades from s Washington to central Oregon.

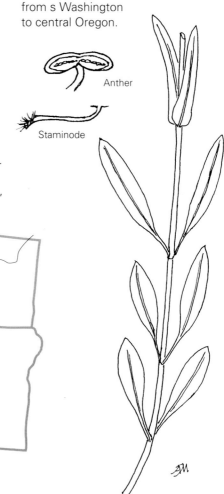

Anther

Staminode

Penstemon
euglaucus

Penstemon euglaucus

80. *PENSTEMON RYDBERGII* A. NELSON
Rydberg's Penstemon

Penstemon rydbergii memorializes Pehr Axel Rydberg (1860–1931), botanist at the New York Botanical Garden and author. This wide-ranging species has acquired numerous names by different authors and now has three recognized varieties, which are included in this book's key. A fourth variety could be segregated in south-central Washington as variety *vaseyanus* on the basis of a few minute teeth on the leaves and somewhat stouter stems than normal.

Stems: Glabrous or minutely pubescent, normally 2 to 7 dm (8–28 in.) tall, with short, sterile shoots present at the base.

Leaves: Basal rosette prominent, the basal leaves oblanceolate or elliptic, 3 to 12 cm (1–4³/₄ in.) long, tapered to short or moderately long petioles, entire and glabrous; cauline leaves relatively few and widely spaced, oblong to lanceolate, 2.5 to 7 cm (1–2³/₄ in.) long, sessile or clasping above.

Inflorescence: Glabrous or finely pubescent, of 1 to 7 crowded, narrow but well-spaced verticillasters, the flowers held horizontal.

Calyx: Quite variable depending on the variety, 3 to 9 mm (to ³/₈ in.) long, the sepals strongly to narrowly scarious, the margins strongly erose-toothed in var. *rydbergii* to mostly entire in var. *oreocharis*.

Corolla: Blue-purple, the tube gradually inflated to the mouth and white or violet at the base, 9 to 15 mm (³/₈–⁵/₈ in.) long, distinctly 2-lipped, the lobes moderately spreading.

Anthers: Glabrous outside, the sacs completely dehiscent, opening to boat-shaped or seldom explanate and spreading opposite.

Staminode: Rarely glabrous to strongly bearded, usually just reaching the orifice.

Blooming: May to July.

Habitat: Usually in meadows to moist, open slopes from the foothills to medium elevations in the mountains.

Range: Central Washington to sw Montana and south along the e Cascades and Sierras to Utah and New Mexico, also the northern end of the Willamette Valley in Oregon and adjacent Washington.

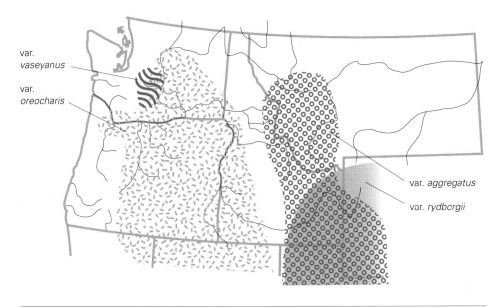

var.
vaseyanus

var.
oreocharis

var. *aggregatus*

var. *rydbergii*

P. rydbergii var. rydbergii

P. rydbergii var. oreocharis

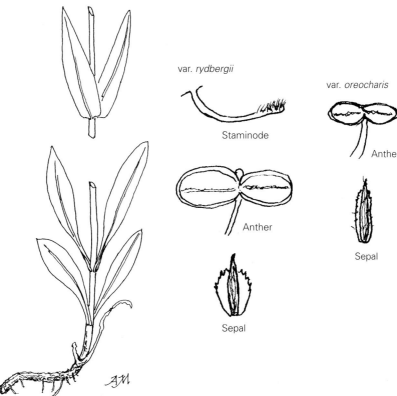

var. *rydbergii*

Staminode

var. *oreocharis*

Anther

Anther

Sepal

Sepal

Word Glossary

acuminate—tapered to a sharp point with concave sides, as a leaf or sepal.

acute—tapered to a sharp point with straight sides.

alternate—arising singly at each node on a stem, as the leaves.

anther—the pollen-producing organ of the stamen; in *Penstemon*, a pair of terminal sacs.

ascending—growing upward obliquely, as stems or flowers on a stem.

basal—growing at the base, as leaves at or near the ground.

beard—a tuft of hairs, as on the palate or staminode.

blade—the broad part of a leaf or petal.

bract—a leaf, usually reduced, in the inflorescence, from the axil of which a floral peduncle or pedicel may arise.

calyx—the sepals of a flower collectively, the outermost portion of a flower.

capsule—a dry specialized seed pod, as in *Penstemon*.

caudate—with a sharp tail-like appendage, as on a leaf tip.

caulescent—with a leafy stem rising above ground.

cauline—of or pertaining to a leafy stem, bearing flowers in *Penstemon*.

channeled—a longitudinal groove, as a leaf folded along the midrib.

clasping—partly or wholly surrounding a stem, as the base of a leaf.

cm (centimeter)—10 millimeters, 0.1 decimeter, 0.01 meter (approx. 13/32 inch).

connate-perfoliate—joined at the base and surrounding a stem, as a pair of leaves.

connective—the tissue joining two pollen sacs as in the stamens of *Penstemon*.

cordate—heart-shaped.

corolla—collectively the petals of a flower; in *Penstemon*, joined at the base to form a tube and the petal lobes.

cyme—one peduncle of a branching inflorescence bearing two or more flowers with the terminal flower blooming first; in *Penstemon*, one side of a verticillaster.

deciduous—with leaves falling at the end of the growing season.

declined—curved or angled downward, i.e., below the horizontal.

decumbent—a stem with a curving or reclining base and erect or ascending tip.

dehiscent—rupturing at maturity, as anther sacs or capsules.

dentate—with spreading or outward-pointing teeth on the margin.

determinate—as an inflorescence in which the terminal flower blooms first, stopping elongation of the peduncle or main stem.

divergent—spreading widely apart but not completely opposite, as the anther sacs in *Penstemon*.

dm (decimeter)—0.1 meter, 10 centimeters, approximately 4 inches.

elliptic—approximately the shape of an oval, as a leaf or sepal.

elongate—growing in length; considerably longer than wide.

endemic—growing in a confined area or geographic region.

entire—continuous, not toothed or cut, as a leaf margin.

erose—a ragged or irregularly cut margin.

evergreen—leaves remaining green over winter.

exotic—introduced; not native to a region.

expanded—enlarged, as the tip of a staminode.

explanate—spreading out flat, as dehiscent anther sacs.

exserted—protruding, as stamens or staminode from a corolla.

fertile—capable of reproduction, as a stamen bearing pollen.

filament—the stalk of a stamen supporting the anther.

fleshy—thick and succulent, pulpy.

flexuous—curved or bent, as a stem.

foliage—the leaves collectively.

genus (pl. genera)—a group of structurally related species; a classification between family and species.

glabrous—a smooth surface; without hairs or glands.

glandular—bearing glands, as on the ends of hairs or on a surface.

glaucous—a fine waxy powder, usually blue or gray, covering a surface.

guide lines—Pigmented veins in the throat or on the palate of a tubular corolla, as in *Penstemon*.

herb—a plant or that part of a plant dying back at the end of a growing season.

herbaceous—green colored, non-woody.

incised—deeply cut, as the teeth on a leaf margin.

inclined—angled upward, above horizontal.

included—enclosed within a structure, as the stamens within the corolla.

indeterminate—as an inflorescence in which the bottom flowers bloom first, so that the peduncle or main stem can continue to elongate.

inflorescence—the flowers collectively on a plant; the arrangement of flowers along a flowering stalk including side branches.

keeled—with a conspicuous longitudinal ridge, as on the top of a corolla.

lanceolate—lance-shaped.

limb—the expanded part of a corolla; from the basal tube to the throat in *Penstemon*.

linear—long and narrow with nearly parallel sides; like a line.

lip—the petals of a corolla aggregated into a shelf, as the upper and lower lips in *Penstemon*.

mm (millimeter)—0.001 meter, approximately 1/25 of an inch.

mucronate—with a short, sharp point at the tip, as a leaf or sepal.

naturalized—introduced into an area and well established.

nectar—a sweet substance produced by a flower to attract pollinating insects; a *nectary* is the structure that produces nectar.

node—the point of attachment of a leaf bract or branch on a stem.

oblanceolate—reverse lance-shaped, attached at the narrow end and enlarged at the outer end.

oblong—Longer than broad with nearly parallel sides, as a leaf.

obtuse—broad at the tip, the sides forming an angle greater than 90 degrees.

opposite—located directly across from each other, as two leaves on a stem or the sacs of a dehiscent anther.

orifice—the mouth or opening of a corolla tube; the throat.

ovary—the expanded base of the pistil; the structure that contains developing seeds in plants.

ovate—broadly elliptic or egg-shaped, as the leaves.

palate—raised portion(s) of the lower lip of the corolla, tending to constrict the throat.

panicle—a branched inflorescence that blooms from the bottom upward.

pedicel—the stalk of a single flower in an inflorescence.

peduncle—the stalk of a cyme or inflorescence or of a single flower.

petiole—a leaf stalk or narrow leaf base.

pistil—the female organ of a flower, typically composed of stigma, style and ovary.

pollen sacs—in *Penstemon*, a pair of pollen sacs constitutes an anther.

prostrate—lying flat on the ground.

pubescent—with hairs of any sort; herein generally hairs without glands.

raceme—an unbranched inflorescence with each flower on an individual pedicel attached to the main axis, blooming from the bottom upward.

reclined—bending or angled downward; lying on some support, as the base of a stem lying on the ground.

recurved—curving or bent backward.

reduced—becoming smaller.

remote—spaced well apart; small in size.

revolute—rolled backward or under, as margins.

rhizome—a horizontal underground stem or rootstock.

robust—vigorous, often above average in size.

rosette—a cluster of leaves, usually encircling the base of a plant.

rotund—round, plump.

sacs—pouches, see *pollen sacs*.

sagittate—in the shape of an arrow or arrowhead.

scarious—thin and white, as the margin of a sepal.

secund—arranged on one side of a main stem, as an inflorescence.

sepals—outermost floral leaves; segments of the calyx.

serrate—like saw teeth; forward-pointing teeth on the margins.

sessile—directly attached at the base, as a leaf without a petiole.

shoots—young or short stems or branches.

shrub—a plant with several stems, woody at the base, not dying back at the base.

spatulate—spatula-shaped, broad and rounded at the end and tapered to a narrow base, as a leaf.

species—a plant that possesses one or more unique characteristics; a classification between genus and variety (subspecies).

spike—an unbranched inflorescence with sessile flowers on the main axis.

spreading—expanding to nearly horizontal branches, as an inflorescence.

stamen—the male, pollen-producing organ of a flower, normally composed of a filament and an anther.

staminode—a modified sterile stamen producing no pollen.

stem—an axis of a plant bearing nodes, leaves and buds, usually above ground.

sterile—not fertile; not producing seeds or pollen; stems without flowers.

stigma—that portion of the pistil on which pollen is deposited, normally the end of the style, often enlarged.

style—the usually slender stalk connecting the stigma and ovary.

sub—a prefix meaning "almost" or "not quite," as in *subequal* and *subshrub*.

suture—a line of fusion or separation, as in the dehiscence of an anther or capsule.

throat—the opening or orifice of a corolla.

thyrse—a densely compact inflorescence; a panicle with indeterminate main axis and cymose branches.

toothed—dentate; having lobes or points along a margin.

truncate—with the end squared off or abruptly rounded as if cut off.

tubular—with the form of a cylinder.

umbel—an inflorescence in which 3 or more pedicels arise from a common point on a stem.

valve—in an anther, one side of the anther wall after dehiscence.

variety—a classification in taxonomy below the species level.

verticillaster—a false whorl; in *Penstemon*, arising at a node and composed of 2 cymes (a branched cluster of blooms that looks like a whorl).

villous—with long, soft hairs.

whorl—a ring of 3 or more leaves or flowers arising from a common node or point.

Illustrated Glossary

Leaves
Leaf Shapes

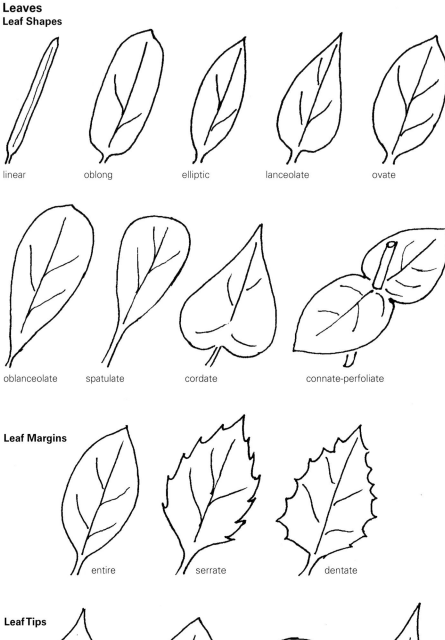

linear   oblong   elliptic   lanceolate   ovate

oblanceolate   spatulate   cordate   connate-perfoliate

Leaf Margins

entire   serrate   dentate

Leaf Tips

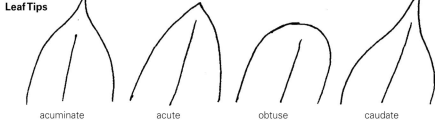

acuminate   acute   obtuse   caudate

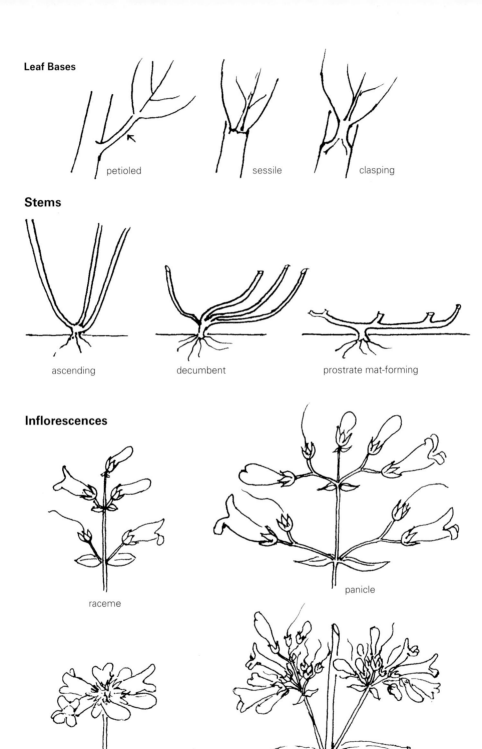

Leaf Bases

petioled   sessile   clasping

Stems

ascending   decumbent   prostrate mat-forming

Inflorescences

raceme

panicle

thyrse

verticillaster (paired cymes)

Selected References

Abrams, L. 1951. *Illustrated Flora of the Pacific States*. Vol. 3. Stanford Univ. Press.

Atwood, N. D., and S. L. Welsh. 1988. An *Erigeron* from Nevada and a *Penstemon* from Idaho. *Great Basin Naturalist* 48:2–495. *(P. idahoensis)*

Backman, S. 1994. Pollination in Penstemons: The Big Three. *Bull. of Am. Penstemon Soc.* No. 53:2–3.

Bennett, R. W. [1960] 1987. *Penstemon Nomenclature*. Revised by K. Lodewick and R. Lodewick. Eugene, OR: Am. Penstemon Soc.

Booth, W. E., and J. C. Wright. 1959. *Flora of Montana, Part II*. Bozeman: Montana State Univ.

Clark, D. V. 1971. Speciation in *Penstemon*. Ph.D. Diss., Univ. of Montana, Missoula.

Cronquist, A., A. Holmgren, N. Holmgren, J. Reveal, and P. Holmgren. 1984. *Intermountain Flora*. 4:370–457. NY Bot. Garden.

Dittberner, P. L., and M. R. Olson. 1983. *The Plant Information Network (PIN): CO, MT, ND, UT and WY*. Washington, D.C.: US Dept. of Interior.

Dorn, R. D. 1984. *Vascular Plants of Montana*. Cheyenne: Mountain West.

_____.1992. *Vascular Plants of Wyoming*. 2d ed. Cheyenne: Mountain West.

Hitchcock, C. L., and A. Cronquist. 1973. *Flora of the Pacific Northwest*. Seattle: Univ. of Washington.

Hitchcock, C. L., A. Cronquist, M. Ownbey, and J. W. Thompson, eds. 1955–1969. *Vascular Plants of the Pacific Northwest*. Vol. 4. Seattle: Univ. of Washington.

Holmgren, N. H. 1991. in Jepson II. *Manual of the Flowering Plants of California*. Berkeley and Los Angeles: Univ. of California Press.

Keck, D. D. 1932. Studies in *Penstemon*. *U of CA Publ. in Botany*. 16:367–425.

_____. 1937. Studies in *Penstemon, Part 4. Bull. of Torrey Bot. Club*. 64:357–81.

_____. 1938. Studies in *Penstemon, Part 6. Bull. of Torrey Bot. Club*. 65:233–55.

_____. 1940. Studies in *Penstemon, Part 7. Am. Midland Naturalist*. 23:594–616.

_____. 1945. Studies in *Penstemon, Part 8. Am. Midland Naturalist*. 33:128–206.

Keck, D. D., and A. Cronquist. 1957. Studies in *Penstemon, Part 9. Brittonia* 8, no. 4:247–50.

Lodewick, K., and R. Lodewick. 1970–1983. *Penstemon Field Identifier*. 9 parts. Eugene, OR. (self-published)

_____. 1991. *Penstemon Notes*. Eugene, OR: Am. Penstemon Soc.

Lodewick, R. 1994. Descriptive Key to Oregon Penstemons. *Kalmiopsis*. Vol. 4. Eugene. Native Plant Soc. of OR. (Also in *Bull. of Am. Penstemon Soc.* 1995. No. 54:2.)

McGregor, R. L., T. M. Barkley, R. E. Brooks, and E. K. Schofield. 1986. *Flora of the Great Plains*. Lawrence: Univ. of Kansas.

Mitchell, D. J. 1748. *Act. Phys. Med. Acad. Nat. Cur.* 8:214.

Munz, P., and D. Keck. 1959. *A California Flora*. Berkeley and Los Angeles: Univ. of California Press.

Peck, M. E. 1961. *Manual of the Higher Plants of Oregon*. Portland: Binford and Morts.

Pennell, F. W. 1920. *Scrophulariaceae of the Central Rocky Mountain States,* US Nat. Herbarium. 20:313–81. GPO.

St. John, H. 1963. *Flora of Southeastern Washington*. Escondido, CA: Edwards Bros.

Straw, R. M. 1956. Floral isolation in *Penstemon. Am. Naturalist*. 90:47–53.

_____. 1966. A Redefinition of *Penstemon. Brittonia* 18:80–95.

Strickler, D. 1993. *Wayside Wildflowers of the Pacific Northwest*. Columbia Falls, MT: Flower Press.

Index

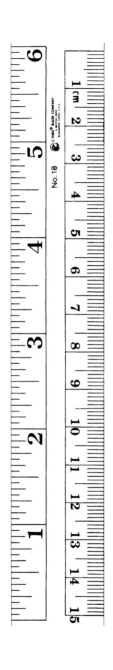